The
American
West

An Illustrated History

LIZ SONNEBORN

A FAIR STREET BOOK

SCHOLASTIC
NONFICTION

Library of Congress Cataloging-in-Publication Data
Sonneborn, Liz.
The American West: An Illustrated History / by Liz Sonneborn.
p. cm.
Includes bibliographical references and index.
1. West (U.S.)—History—Juvenile literature. [1. West (U.S.)—History.]
I. Title.
F591 .S669 2002
978—dc21   2001020938

ISBN 0-439-21970-1

Produced by Fair Street Productions
Editor: Deborah Bull
Designer: Barbara Balch
Photo research coordinator: Shaie Dively

Cover photo: PhotoDisc
All other art permissions appear on page 144.

10 9 8 7 6 5 4 3 2   03 04 05 06 07
Printed in the U.S.A.   24
First printing, October 2002

CONTENTS

INTRODUCTION

Cowboys driving their cattle over the open range. Outlaws and lawmen facing one another on a dusty Main Street. Indian hunters racing through buffalo herds on horseback. These images, so familiar from movies and books, are what come to mind when many people think of the American West. But the real story of the West goes far beyond cowboys and gunfighters. It is the story of many peoples who, over many centuries, came to the region looking for many different things. Lakota warriors, Spanish conquistadors, German farmers, African-American cowboys, Mormon settlers, Chilean miners, Chinese railroad workers—these are only a few of the people who have been lured to the West by its seeming promise of a new and better life.

Where is the American West? The question has no single answer. Unlike a state or a country, the West does not have set boundaries. At different times, it has been defined in different ways. In this book, the words *American West* describe the area of the United States west of the Mississippi River. Including more than half the country, it is a region of many landscapes, from dry deserts to magnificent mountains to lush forests to grassy plains.

But the American West is more than just a place. It is also an idea. The West has always been a symbol of new and exciting possibilities. When people thought about the West, they thought about fresh starts and second chances. If they were poor, unhappy, or restless, they believed they could always head west and begin their lives again. In the American imagination, the open spaces of the region seemed to make a promise: There, the sky truly was the limit.

Some people who moved west saw their dreams come true. A miner might have a lucky strike and discover enough gold to make him rich for life. A farmer might make a comfortable home and good living for his family. A cowboy might find adventure and the freedom to live as he chose. But just as many people who came west watched their dreams fade. Miners went bust, farmers lost their crops to bad weather, and cowboys grew weary of their long hours and low pay. The story of the West, then, is a complicated one—of winners and losers, of success and failure, of triumph and disappointment.

And the story continues to unfold. More than half of the American population now lives west of the Mississippi, and people continue to move there in record numbers. Some come looking for fortune in the computer industry, others for a shot at fame in Hollywood, and still others for clear skies and lovely scenery. People's reasons for flocking west now are different from those of immigrants centuries ago. But one thing remains true: As in the past, the American West, both real and imagined, is still a place that inspires dreams.

◀ *Opposite page:*
Dancing at Glacier Point, Yosemite, California, in the 1890s

CHAPTER ONE

THE FIRST WESTERNERS

About 50,000 B.C. to A.D. 1527

Majestic mountains, crystal-clear rivers, vast grasslands, lush forests, rich soil—these gifts of the land drew immigrants to the American West for centuries. Some came to explore, some to settle, some to make their fortunes, and some merely for adventure. Whatever their reasons, many newcomers shared the same experience upon seeing the western landscape for the first time. They looked at the West as though they were discovering a new world, one to conquer and make their own.

The Ancient Ones

The region, however, was hardly new to one group. Long before any of these immigrants arrived, the first westerners—American Indian people from hundreds of different tribes—had made the West their home.

Western Indian tribes tell sacred tales, called creation stories, to explain how they came to live in their homelands. Archaeologists (experts who study the remains of ancient human societies) have developed scientific theories of how people first arrived in the American West. One well-known theory is that the first people came to North America from northeast Asia sometime between

◀ *Opposite page:*
Ancient Indian drawings
discovered in Wyoming

CREATION STORIES

Many Indians do not believe their ancestors came from Asia along the Bering Land Bridge. For the earliest history of their people, they instead turn to the creation story of their tribe. These sacred narratives tell how the world was created and how the first people came to be. Here are just a few stories told by western Indians about the beginnings of humankind.

The Modoc of Oregon and California recount the story of Kumush, who traveled to the underworld with his daughter. There he collected the bones of spirits in a large basket, which he brought to the earth. He divided the bones into groups, each of which became a different tribe. The bravest spirits became the Modoc.

The Diegueño of California say that Tu-chai-pai, the Maker, created the world. After making hills, rivers, and forests, he dug up some mud and shaped it into the first humans.

The Zuni, who live in New Mexico, believe that humans were made by Mother Earth and Father Sky. The first people had to travel up through four underworlds before emerging in the Zuni homeland.

The Jicarilla Apache of New Mexico tell of Black Hacticin, who drew a figure on the ground in his own image. He placed pollen and stones on the outline to form flesh and blood. After a gust of wind gave the figure breath, the first human came to life.

This clay sculpture made by twentieth-century Cochiti Pueblo artist Helen Cordero depicts an Indian storyteller surrounded by an audience of children.

50,000 B.C. and 10,000 B.C. Most likely, these early humans were hunters who followed large game animals over the Bering Land Bridge—a strip of land that once connected Asia to Alaska but is now covered with water. Gradually, these humans—the ancestors of the peoples now called Indians—moved farther and farther south. Eventually,

these early humans were living throughout the Americas.

When humans crossed the Bering Land Bridge, the earth was experiencing a series of ice ages. The climate was so cold that much of the ground was covered with glaciers, great patches of ice. Slowly, the temperature began to rise. Although the warming of the earth made more areas livable for humans, the higher temperatures probably helped kill off the elephantlike mastodons, woolly mammoths, and saber-toothed tigers that once lived in North America. As big-game hunters, humans relied on these huge animals for meat to eat and for furs to wear. When they died off, people had to look for new sources of food. Increasingly, their diet included wild plants, fish, and meat from small animals.

About eight thousand years ago, Indians in Mexico began feeding themselves in a new way—by growing their own food. They first learned to grow beans, squash, and avocados. But the crop most important to their survival was maize, or Indian corn. Wild corn had tiny ears with few kernels. By breeding it with wild grasses, though, early Indians discovered they could grow hardier plants with bigger, better-tasting kernels.

Slowly, knowledge of how to grow corn spread northward to Indians living in the American West. For some western Indians, the introduction of corn had little impact. In present-day California, so many wild plants were available to eat that Indians did not need to grow more. Similarly, along the Pacific Coast in what are now Oregon and Washington, people could get all the food they needed by fishing. In the hot and dry desert lands of the Southwest, though, growing corn offered Indians the best way to obtain the food they needed.

As southwest Indians came to rely on farmed foods, their lives changed. While Indians who hunted animals and gathered plants lived in small bands and traveled wherever they could find food, the Indian farmers of the Southwest had to settle in one place so they could tend to their fields. Farming also allowed their populations to increase. Once the Indians knew how to grow crops, they could feed more people. Over the course of thousands of years, small settlements grew into huge villages. About two thousand years ago, these villagers started developing distinct ways of life, or distinct cultures.

One of the three great early Indian cultures in the Southwest was that of the Mogollon, whose settlements were located in the mountainous area of present-day southern Arizona and New Mexico. The Mogollon are best known for their pottery. Made to store corn and carry water, their pots were works of art. The greatest Mogollon potters lived in the Mimbres Valley, and Mimbres pottery featured black designs painted on a white background. Pots decorated with animal designs have been found in old Mogollon grave sites. Before burying them, the Mogollon punched

These sixteenth-century illustrations show Mexican Indians planting corn and tending their fields.

A tool used by the Pomo Indians of California to gather seeds

PICTURING THE WEST

The grandest building at Chaco Canyon was Pueblo Bonito. Built by the Anasazi between A.D. 800 and 1100, it was given its name by Spanish explorers, who first saw it in the sixteenth century. Although much of the building had been destroyed, the Spaniards were so amazed by its ruins that they called it "Beautiful Town" in their language. At its height, Pueblo Bonito had eight hundred separate rooms arranged in a D-shape around a great open plaza. The Anasazi used more than one million adobe bricks in its construction. Until the nineteenth century, Pueblo Bonito was the largest building ever made in the United States.

holes in the pots to free the animals' spirits so they could guide the dead to the afterworld.

Living in what is now southern Arizona, to the west of the Mogollon, were the Hohokam. These people were particularly clever farmers who irrigated their land by digging ditches to draw water from nearby rivers directly to their fields. Today, visitors can see the ruins of one of their villages, now known as Snaketown, near Phoenix, Arizona. It housed a great ball court where ancient Indians gathered to play a game similar to soccer. Early cultures in Mexico also built ball courts, which makes some anthropologists (scientists who study human societies) believe the Hohokam had contact with peoples living far to the south. Possibly, the Hohokam traded with Mexican Indians for brightly colored feathers, turquoise, copper bells, conch shells, and other luxury items.

Perhaps the greatest early southwestern culture was that of the Hisatsinom, or as they are called by their descendants, the Hopi. They are known more widely as the Anasazi, a name that means variously "ancient ones" or "enemies of our ancient fathers" in the Navajo language. The Anasazi lived in the Four Corners area, where the borders of present-day Arizona, Utah, Colorado, and New Mexico meet. They occupied many villages, which were connected by 250 miles of roads. To trade food and other goods, Anasazi from different villages gathered at Chaco Canyon, an enormous trade center that had a population of more than five thousand people.

In their villages, the Anasazi constructed dwellings made of adobe, or dried clay. An adobe house started with

one room. Then rooms were added by building three walls around an outside wall of the original house. Rooms were also built on the roof to add a second story. Over time, an adobe structure could become large enough to house an entire village.

The Anasazi also used adobe to construct cliff dwellings. These amazing houses were built into the walls of cliffs, and to reach them, the inhabitants had to climb up the cliff face using hand and foot holes cut for this purpose. Getting to a cliff dwelling was so difficult that the residents were afforded protection from their enemies. Today, at the site of Mesa Verde in southwest Colorado, are the ruins of Cliff Palace, a huge cliff dwelling containing more than two hundred rooms. Baron Gustaf

Detail from a thirteenth-century Mimbres pot

A water jar made by southwestern Indians in about 1200

The Pueblo village of Oraibi

Nordenskjöld, the first scientist to study Cliff Palace, wrote in 1891 that "with its round towers and high walls rising out of the heaps of stones . . . it resembles at a distance an enchanted castle."

Although some of their buildings still stand, the Anasazi, Mogollon, and Hohokam centers had all but disappeared by 1300. No one knows for sure what happened to these early peoples; most likely, droughts or other climate changes made it impossible for them to grow enough food to feed themselves. Over time, they abandoned their fields and large villages, moving off in small groups in search of other sources of food.

Pueblo and Navajo

Descendants of the Anasazi probably became the Pueblo. The Pueblo were not an Indian tribe, but were instead many different peoples who had similar languages and ways of life. Clustered along the Rio Grande Valley in what is now central New Mexico, they lived in villages of adobe houses. Although Pueblo villages traded with one another, each functioned as an independent nation. Beginning in the sixteenth century, Spaniards used the

Spanish word *pueblo* ("town") to describe both such a village and the people who lived in it.

Like their Anasazi ancestors, the Pueblo were farmers who grew corn, beans, and squash. Located along the Rio Grande, their lands were better-watered than most areas of the dry Southwest. Still, they had to work hard to irrigate their fields and when rainfall levels were very low, there was little they could do to save their harvest. Entire villages could starve in years of drought.

To cope with the uncertainty in their lives, the Pueblo came to depend on one another. At a young age, they were taught that the needs of just one person were of little importance. Instead, a good Pueblo was expected to sacrifice his or her own desires and do what was best for the group.

To protect themselves from hard times, the Pueblo also looked to spirit beings called kachinas. Through religious ceremonies, the Pueblo asked the kachinas for help. There were several hundred kachinas, each with its own name and powers. To teach girls about the kachinas, Pueblo parents gave them wooden dolls carved to represent these spirits.

The Pueblo also had to guard themselves against Indian enemies. By about 1400 the Navajo and the Apache had begun arriving in the Southwest. Hundreds of years ago, they probably lived far to the north, possibly in what is now Canada. The languages and ways of these newcomers were very different from those of the Pueblo. Instead of being settled farmers, they were wandering hunters and gatherers. In the Southwest, though, there were few wild animals and plants; to survive, the Navajo and Apache took to raiding Pueblo settlements and stealing their hard-earned corn.

Despite their new setting, the Apache clung to their old way of life. The Navajo, however, began to change. Probably by watching the Pueblo, they slowly discovered how to farm in their new homeland and also learned new skills, such as weaving. In time, the Navajo were even performing their own versions of Pueblo ceremonies.

The Navajo's skill at blending old and new ways changed their lives even more after non-Indians began coming to the Southwest in the mid-sixteenth century. They quickly learned to raise horses and sheep, animals non-Indians

Western Voices

"What we are told as children is that people when they walk on the land leave their breath wherever they go. So wherever we walk, that particular spot on the earth never forgets us, and when we go back to these places, we know that the people who have lived there are in some way still there, and that we can actually partake of their breath and of their spirit."

—*Santa Clara Pueblo Rina Swentzell, on her people's connection to their homeland*

The Fourth World

The Navajo say that their people traveled through three underworlds before coming to live on the surface of the earth. Some anthropologists believe this ancient story mirrors their theory that the Navajo came to the Southwest from lands far to the north. In their view, each world represents an area the tribe passed through during their migration south. The first, the Black World, is the cold, dark, Arctic region. The second, the Blue-Green World, is the forest lands of Canada. The third, the Yellow World, is the plains east of the Rocky Mountains. And the final one, the Glittering World, is the Navajo homeland in northwestern New Mexico.

A kachina doll

The Lizard Eaters

Neighboring the abundant homelands of the California Indians was the Great Basin. This desert area, centered in present-day Utah and Nevada, also included parts of what are now Colorado, Wyoming, and Idaho. With almost no rainfall and temperatures rising as high as 140 degrees, few living things could survive there. Yet resourceful Indian peoples such as the Ute, Paiute, and Shoshone made this area their home.

These Indians spent each day in search of food and water. Women gathered roots and the nuts of the piñon tree, one of the few plants that grew above ground. Using bows and arrows, men hunted small birds, squirrels, rabbits, and raccoons.

Lizards, snakes, and insects provided the Indians with a good meal when nothing else was available. In the nineteenth century, non-Indians often called them "lizard eaters." But for the Great Basin tribes, developing a taste for these unusual foods was often their best hope for survival.

introduced to the region. With these new talents, the Navajo emerged as the best Indian ranchers in the West.

The California Indians

To the northwest of the Pueblo and Navajo lived the native peoples of California. Before the sixteenth century, as many as 300,000 Indians dwelled in this region, accounting for nearly a third of all native people then living in the present-day United States and Canada.

The population of California grew so large because it was by comparison easy to live there. The climate was mild year-round, so weather rarely threatened anyone's survival. Indians in California knew little of the scorching summer heat or the bitter winter cold that regularly endangered people living in harsher environments.

Food was also plentiful in California, and Indians could gather a wide array of tasty fruits and vegetables—from grapes and berries to wild seeds, bulbs, and roots. They could also hunt quail, rabbits, and deer

and fish for trout and salmon. For those living near oak trees, the most important food was acorns. In autumn, families gathered in the oak forests for the annual harvest. Boys climbed the trees and shook the branches, and as the acorns fell on the ground below, women and children grabbed them up and threw them into great baskets they carried on their backs. If properly stored, the nuts would stay fresh for a year. Pounded into a flour and baked, they were used to make bread. Another favorite dish was a mush made from pounded acorns, water, and berries.

Because of the region's richness, California Indians enjoyed far more comfortable lives than most native peoples. For instance, the Pueblo, despite all their hard work in their fields, might still not have had enough food. The California peoples, on the other hand, could rely on nature to provide whatever they needed. Still, they did what they could to insure that their harvest of wild foods would be as great as possible. Young women, for instance, were careful when gathering the bulbs of hyacinth plants, which covered California meadows with beautiful white and purple-blue flowers. They collected only the largest bulbs,

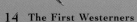

which they then baked and fed to their families. To be sure of a good harvest the next year, they replanted any small bulbs they dug up. And to keep the wild hyacinth plants healthy, the women poked holes in the ground with sticks to let air and water reach the roots.

Food was so plentiful in the land around them that the California Indians had little reason to travel far from home. Although they sometimes traded with nearby groups, most had little contact with people outside their own small villages. In mountainous regions, where villages were particularly isolated, Indians could easily pass their lives without ever meeting an outsider. Because they had so little interaction with others, groups of villages over time developed their own unique languages. By about 1500, the Indians of California

spoke about one hundred languages and several hundred dialects.

Even though they lived in many different small bands and tribes, California Indians existed almost free of conflict. Each village was able to meet its own needs, so people did not have to fight one another for territory or for food. Their environment also kept foreign Indians out. Potential invaders were blocked to the west by the ocean, to the east by the mountains, and to the south by the desert. Until the eighteenth century, the California Indians were largely left to themselves to enjoy the fruits of their lush surroundings.

A woman of the Hupa tribe preparing a meal from acorns in the early twentieth century

A basket made by the Pomo Indians

People of Salmon and Cedar

California Indians were fortunate to live in a land of plenty. But perhaps even luckier were the native peoples to their north. Indian groups such as the Haida, Chinook, Makah, Tlingit, Coast Salish, and Kwakiutl (also known as the Kwakwaka'wakw) occupied the lush lands along the coast of present-day western Oregon, Washington, and British Columbia. The region was a comfortable place. The moderate climate was never too hot or too cold. Although it rained much of the year, the damp weather was a blessing that helped keep the river waters high and allowed all kinds of plants and trees to flourish.

Tall cedar trees gave the Northwest Coast peoples the materials to make almost everything they needed. They cut the trees into planks and built large rectangular houses to shield them from the rain, wove flexible strips of bark to make clothing and baskets, and carved the trunks into canoes to navigate

A wooden rattle made by the Tlingit

both the ocean and the many rivers that flowed through their lands.

Although the Northwest Coast Indians hunted deer and elk and gathered wild fruits and berries, nearly all their food came from nearby waters. Walking along the beach, they could gather basketfuls of oysters and mussels that washed ashore. Using cleverly crafted hooks, spears, and nets, they could catch all the fresh trout they could eat. Their most important food, though, was salmon. The rivers were so full of these fish that the Northwest Coast Indians could easily survive by eating salmon alone.

Every spring, families would camp along the edge of rivers for the salmon run—the fishes' annual trip upstream to lay their eggs. During the run, the rivers were literally overflowing with fish, and people needed only to scoop a net through the water to collect a fantastic

day's catch. After feasting on fresh fish throughout the spring, the Indians still had plenty of salmon left. Women dried and smoked the surplus so it could be eaten later. The Indians could catch and preserve so many fish that working only a few weeks during the salmon season provided enough food for the rest of the year.

With their food needs taken care of, the Northwest Coast peoples had months of leisure time that they could spend preparing for and performing an elaborate series of winter rituals. During these ceremonies, performers danced, sang, and acted out stories of the spirit beings who controlled the universe.

Many Northwest Coast Indians also held and attended potlatches, great feasts that were hosted by the wealthiest and most powerful families in their villages. No one is certain when these peoples first started holding potlatches, though some anthropologists

A potlatch held in British Columbia, Canada, in 1859

A salmon carved from soapstone by the Coast Salish

A Tlingit coat woven from cedar bark, mountain goat wool, and fur.

gifts—blankets, canoes, even slaves. The Northwest Coast Indians believed that the more people gave away, the more respect they would receive from their neighbors. If guests left pleased with their lavish gifts, the potlatch was a success. The host family could be sure that no one would question their position of power and privilege for years to come.

Plateau and Plains

To the east of the Northwest Coast nations were the natives of the Columbia River Plateau, in what are now eastern Oregon and Washington and western Idaho. This expanse of high, level land was sandwiched between two great mountain ranges, and tribes including the Nez Percé, Yakima, Umatilla, and Walla Walla told their children stories about how they came to live in the region. In their legends, a character named Coyote had prepared this land just for them. Before humans arrived on the plateau, Coyote killed the Swallowing Monster that lived in the Columbia River. He then scattered the monster's bones and blood, forming the beautiful landscape around them.

Like their coastal neighbors, the Plateau Indians relied on salmon for most of their food. In April, as the salmon run began, they left their villages to gather at the Dalles, an area along the Columbia River. There, at a series of rapids, fishers could easily catch the salmon as they headed upriver. Meeting at the Dalles each year also gave the

consider the potlatch a fairly new custom. They believe potlatches were performed only after non-Indian traders came to the Northwest Coast in the late eighteenth century.

A potlatch often commemorated an important event, such as a marriage or the death of a prominent person. But nearly any occasion—even a baby's first haircut—could become an excuse for one. The real purpose behind a potlatch was to let the host family show off their wealth and remind everyone of their high social status.

The potlatch hosts provided plenty of entertainment for their guests. In addition to a fine meal, they enjoyed songs, dances, and speeches. But the most exciting part of the festivities was the giveaway. At an elaborate potlatch, hosts offered their guests all kinds of

Plateau Indians a chance to trade and visit with one another, and these regular get-togethers kept people of different tribes friendly. Although they sometimes fought Indians from other regions, Plateau peoples rarely warred with one another.

In mid-June the Indians again left their villages, this time setting out for the prairies. There, under the earth, was the Plateau tribes' other staple food—camas root. They found the roots by poking holes in the ground with pointed digging sticks. Even though digging for camas was hard work, the Indians looked forward to spending time in their summer camps, where they visited old friends, traded for new goods, and played games together.

As the heat rose in late summer, many people escaped to the mountains, where they spent the fall gathering berries and hunting deer. Men sometimes headed east to spend the season in the Great Plains, a flat, grassy region in the middle of the United States. On the Plains, they joined the Indians living there in hunting buffalo.

Buffalo hunting was then just a small part of the Plains Indians' way of life. Most Plains peoples were farmers who lived in villages near their fields, which were located in riverbeds. Farming, however, was a risky business on the Plains. Probably in the late thirteenth century, the region suffered a severe drought. With so little water, few plants could grow, and the population on the Plains fell sharply. The people who remained lived in villages clustered along the Missouri—the great river that snakes through the northern Plains.

Within three centuries, though, a new way of life would come to the Plains. The peoples who dominated the region would no longer be settled farmers, but great hunters and warriors who spent their lives roaming the grasslands. This change was only one of many that Indians would face as non-Indians arrived in the West.

A nineteenth-century illustration of a buffalo herd

A pair of Umatilla moccasins decorated with beads

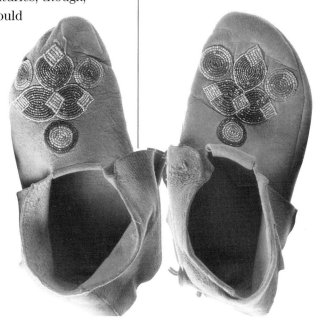

CHAPTER TWO

CULTURES CLASH

1528 to 1802

In 1492, on an expedition funded by the Spanish king, Ferdinand, and Queen Isabella, Italian explorer Christopher Columbus and his crew became the first Europeans to travel to North America. Soon after, Spain began sending soldiers called *conquistadors* to the continent to search for gold and other riches. By the early 1500s Spanish colonies, or settlements, had appeared in Mexico and on the Caribbean islands. Spain then began eyeing lands in Florida.

The Seven Cities of Cíbola

In 1528 a Spanish expedition to Florida met with terrible luck. Its crew endured two brutal storms, and only four men survived. Shipwrecked on the coast of the Gulf of Mexico, they were rescued and taken in by the Karankawa Indians, with whom the Spaniards lived for six years. The survivors then decided to head overland to the Spanish colony in Mexico. The six-thousand-mile journey took them through present-day Texas, New Mexico, and Arizona. They were the first non-Indians to travel through the American Southwest.

Once in Mexico, one of the men, Álvar Núñez Cabeza de Vaca, wrote of his

◄ *Opposite page: This nineteenth-century Indian drawing, found on a canyon wall in Arizona, depicts Spanish horsemen.*

The Cabrilho-Ferrelo Expedition

While Coronado was traveling through the Southwest, another explorer, Portuguese-born navigator João Rodriques Cabrilho, was mapping the Pacific shore for the Spanish crown. In 1542 Cabrilho led an expedition of three ships up the coast of present-day California. He and his men became the first non-Indians to see the areas where cities such as San Diego and Los Angeles would later grow up. During the expedition, Cabrilho died, but his pilot, Bartolomé Ferrelo, carried on. He took the ships all the way to the northern border of what is now California before turning back to Mexico. Because of Cabrilho's and Ferrelo's travels, Spain held claim to California for almost three hundred years.

Treasures, such as this Aztec turquoise-and-shell serpent, made Spanish conquistadors hungry for the riches of the Americas.

adventures in a book titled *Naufragios* (Spanish for "shipwrecks"). In it, Cabeza de Vaca described the Indian people he met and the plants and animals he saw. But far more interesting to the Spanish conquistadors were his tales of the riches north of Mexico. According to Cabeza de Vaca, his Indian friends told him of fabulous cities there that contained great wealth.

The stories reminded the Spaniards of Tenochtitlán, in central Mexico. In 1521 conquistador Hernando Cortés and his army had invaded this beautiful and wealthy city, the capital of the Aztec Indian empire, and destroyed it, slaughtering its residents and stealing their gold and other prized possessions. Once the Aztec were defeated, the Spaniards enslaved the surviving Indians and forced them to mine precious metals that made their conquerors rich.

To confirm Cabeza de Vaca's tale of riches to the north, the Spanish authorities sent out a small party from Mexico headed by Marcos de Niza, a Catholic priest. The party's guide was Estevanico, a black slave who had been shipwrecked with Cabeza de Vaca. Traveling ahead of the rest, Estevanico reached Hawikuh, a village of the Zuni Pueblo near what is now Albuquerque,

New Mexico. Immediately, he demanded women and riches. Just as quickly, the Zuni responded by killing him.

Before scurrying back to Mexico, de Niza caught a quick glimpse of Hawikuh. When asked what he had seen, he let his imagination get the better of him. With his own eyes, de Niza claimed, he had seen one of the seven great cities described by Cabeza de Vaca. Calling the village Cíbola, de Niza said it was

bigger than Mexico City, Mexico's (New Spain's) capital, and filled with ten-story buildings covered with turquoise. He called it "the greatest and the best" settlement the Spaniards had yet seen in North America.

The report gave the Spanish all the encouragement they needed. Leading three hundred Spanish soldiers and eight hundred Mexican Indians, Francisco Vásquez de Coronado headed north from Mexico up an old Indian trail. On July 7, 1540, Coronado's army reached Hawikuh. Although the Zuni fought to keep them out, the Spanish force defeated them and conquered the village. Any pleasure the Spaniards took in their victory, though, faded as they searched in vain for the great stashes of gold they had imagined. They found nothing but, as one soldier wrote, "stone and mud."

The disappointed Spanish expedition remained in Hawikuh for four months. During their stay, the conquistadors brutalized the Zuni while constantly demanding food and supplies. Still

convinced there was gold in the region, Coronado sent his men off in all directions. One group found the Grand Canyon. Another explored the Great Plains, where the men became the first Europeans to see buffalo. (The Spaniards called the unfamiliar animals "shaggy cows.") But no one discovered the gold of Coronado's dreams.

A 1902 illustration by American artist Frederic Remington shows the Coronado expedition's march into Pueblo territory.

This picture of a buffalo was based on descriptions of the animal made by early Spanish explorers in the West.

*An 1883 photograph
of the Pueblo village
of Acoma*

As winter set in, the Spaniards finally gave up hope. They trudged home, leaving the relieved Zuni once again in command of Hawikuh. In Mexico Coronado's expedition was considered a complete disaster. For the next 40 years, no Spaniard could see any good reason for retracing his steps.

The Pueblo Revolt

Still, among the Spanish, the dream of riches in Pueblo territory never quite died. In 1595 Don Juan de Oñate,

the son of a wealthy miner, decided he could succeed where Coronado had failed. He convinced King Philip II to let him build a Spanish colony north of Mexico. Oñate wanted to call his colony Nuevo Mexico, or New Mexico.

In 1598, with about 130 men and their families, Oñate arrived in the lands of the Pueblo. He rode from village to village, announcing that the Indians were now subjects of the Spanish king. Unfamiliar with Spanish, the Indians had no idea what he was saying. But they clearly understood that these outsiders wanted to take over their villages.

Most of the Pueblo resisted the Spaniards, but the invaders met the strongest hostility at Acoma, a village set atop a 356-foot-high mesa. There men shot arrows and women threw rocks as the Spanish army approached. Oñate responded by telling his men to attack the inhabitants and destroy their houses. Although the Spaniards were outnumbered, the Indians' weapons were no match for European guns. The Spanish army killed eight hundred Acoma Indians before the fighting was over.

After defeating the Indians of Acoma, conquistador Juan de Oñate took more than five hundred men, women, and children captive. He decided to use them to send a message to the other Pueblo peoples and sentenced all captives older than twelve to 20 years as slaves. Men older than twenty-five were given an additional punishment: One of their feet was cut off in a gruesome public ceremony. Oñate also ordered his men to sever one hand each of two Hopi men who happened to be visiting Acoma when the fighting broke out. He then set the mutilated Hopi free so other Indians could see what might happen if they defied the Spaniards. Hearing of the Acoma massacre, the other Pueblo villages reluctantly accepted Spanish rule to avoid a similar fate.

In the search for gold, however, Oñate had no better luck than Coronado. His colonists soon realized they would not find great riches in the Pueblo's land and settled instead for putting the Pueblo people to work for them. The Spaniards insisted that the Indians give them a portion of the corn crop they worked hard to grow. Often the Pueblo did not have enough corn for themselves, so having to feed the Spanish invaders too was a great hardship.

The situation grew worse as they had more contact with the Spaniards.

The colonists brought European diseases such as measles and smallpox, which previously were unknown in the region. Although the Spanish people had developed natural defenses against these illnesses, the Indians had not. Many Pueblo died, leaving fewer and fewer to work the fields.

The Spaniards also angered the Pueblo by trying to convert them to Catholicism. Among Oñate's settlers were about 30 priests, who told the Pueblo that their own religion was evil and that their souls would be lost unless they became Christians. The priests forced the Indians to build churches and work as servants, often beating anyone who refused. The Pueblo's fury grew as the priests began destroying masks and other ceremonial objects and harassing their holy men. In 1675 the Spanish authorities arrested 47 of the Pueblo's most respected religious leaders and charged them with sorcery. Four were sentenced to hang, and the rest were whipped.

The Aztec in this illustration are dying from smallpox, a disease the Spaniards introduced to the American West.

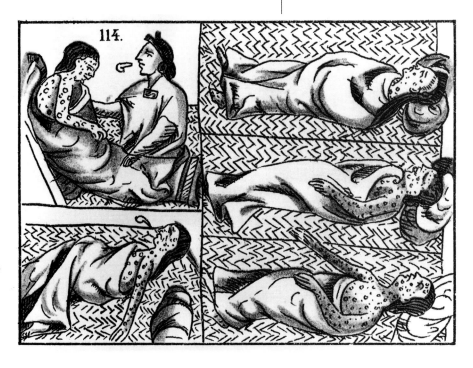

Fr Angel.   *Fr Martin de Jesus.*   *El Rey Azayatl.*   *Ziguangua Cuinieranguari y Zintzun*   *sus mugeres*

This drawing from the mid-eighteenth century shows two priests preaching to four Mexican Indians. The Spanish similarly tried to convert western Indians to Catholicism.

Among the survivors was Popé, a leader from the village of San Juan in present-day New Mexico. The experience left him with a hatred of all things Spanish, and he set about persuading the Pueblo to band together to force the invaders from their lands. This was no easy task. The Pueblo occupied as many as 50 separate villages that operated independently and often fought with one another. Persuading all the villages to work together was almost impossible, but as the Spanish abuses continued, Popé rallied more and more followers to his cause.

In mid-August 1680 Popé was ready. He sent word to the Spanish that they should leave. Most, of course, ignored his warning. Then, all at once, the Pueblo of each village rose up against the Spaniards in their midst and killed about four hundred colonists, including some twenty priests. About two thousand Spaniards escaped and fled south to Mexico. Carefully planned and executed, the Pueblo Revolt was the most successful Indian uprising in history.

After the Spanish colonists were gone, Popé's followers began destroying everything they had left behind. They wrecked homes, tore down churches, and killed livestock. Popé told all those who had been baptized by the priests to scrub their bodies clean. He also insisted that no Pueblo ever use anything the Spaniards had brought into their villages. Many Indians resisted this order because during the 80 years of Spanish rule, the Pueblo had been introduced to many European goods and products that had improved their lives. They did not want to give up useful European animals, such as cattle and sheep, and delicious European foods, such as wheat, oats, peaches, and plums. Because many Pueblo refused to follow Popé's rules, his power faded. Soon the Pueblo were no longer a united people. Each village went back to being ruled by its own leaders.

In 1692 a Spanish expedition returned to Pueblo territory. Led by Diego de Vargas, soldiers fought the Indians for six years before subduing them. But this time things were different for both the Spaniards and the Pueblo.

Western Voices

"[Popé said] that we should burn all the images and temples, rosaries and crosses and that all the people should discard the names given them in holy baptism. . . . [W]e were not to mention in any manner the name of God, of the . . . Virgin, or of the Saints . . . [and were] not to teach the [Spanish] language in any pueblo and to burn the seeds which the Spaniards sowed and to plant only [corn] and beans, which are the crops of our ancestors."

—*Tesuque Indian Juan, on the Pueblo Revolt of 1680*

Having learned a lesson from the Pueblo Revolt, the Spanish colonists treated the Indians less harshly and demanded much less labor from them. The priests still tried to convert them, but when the Pueblo persisted in practicing their traditional religion, the priests stopped fighting their holy men and just began looking the other way.

The Pueblo too developed more patience in dealing with the Spaniards, meeting the foreigners' demands as long as the colonists continued to supply them with European goods. They also came to welcome the Spaniards as military allies. Together the Pueblo and Spanish settlers fought to keep Navajo and Apache Indians from stealing corn from the Pueblo's villages. Although the Pueblo and Spaniards were never

wholly comfortable with each other, they found a way to share the same land in peace for the next 150 years.

Horses and Warriors

According to Cheyenne Indian tradition, a prophet named Sweet Medicine once dwelled among the tribe. Over four lifetimes, he taught the Cheyenne of the Great Plains how to live and how to perform ceremonies to honor the Creator. Before dying, Sweet Medicine gathered the Cheyenne people and said they would soon experience great changes. He told them they would encounter a beast with a shaggy neck

Buffalo Hunting

Many Plains Indians had been buffalo hunters even before they had horses. Stalking a buffalo on foot, though, was dangerous work. To sneak up on one of the huge animals, hunters often crept on all fours, wearing the skin of a wolf to disguise themselves. Once they got close enough, they killed their prey with spears. After horses came to the Plains, hunters more often used bows and arrows.

Two Plains Indian hunters, hidden in wolf skins, sneak up on a herd of buffalo in this painting by American artist George Catlin in 1832–1833.

The Palace of the Governors

In 1609 Spain ordered Don Pedro de Peralta, the third governor of the New Mexico colony, to build a town that could serve as the colonial capital. Using Mexican Indians as laborers, he oversaw the construction of Santa Fe ("Holy Faith") on the site of ancient Indian ruins. The town featured a central plaza surrounded by a church and several government buildings; the grandest was the Palace of the Governors, where Peralta and his successors were to live. It is the oldest European building still standing in the United States. For three centuries, it was used by officials of the three countries—Spain, Mexico, and the United States—that claimed Santa Fe during this period. Since 1909 the Palace of the Governors has been open to the public as a branch of the Museum of New Mexico.

Crafted by a Lakota Sioux artist, this wooden horse was probably used during ceremonial dances held to celebrate Lakota war victories.

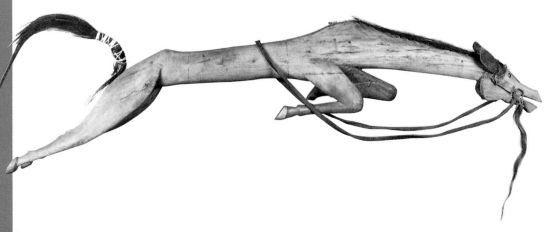

Spaniards using pulleys to hoist a horse onto a ship bound for North America

and a long tail that nearly touched the ground. "This animal," the prophet said, "will carry you on his back and help you in many ways. Those far hills that seem only a blue vision in the distance take many days to reach now; but with this animal you can get there in a short time, so fear him not."

The animal in Sweet Medicine's prophecy was the horse. In prehistoric times, a species of horse had lived in North America. But about ten thousand

years ago, these horses died out. The horses the Cheyenne would ride were brought to the West from Europe by the Spanish explorers. Over time, some of these horses escaped their masters and began to roam free in wild herds. Others were stolen by Indian raiders. By about 1700, horses were commonly found on the grassy lands of the Great Plains.

The horse was a boon to the Indians of the Plains. As Sweet Medicine had predicted, riding horses enabled people to travel great distances faster than ever before. Strong and sturdy, the animals could also carry heavy loads from place to place. Best of all, on horseback hunters could more easily follow the buffalo herds that wandered the Plains.

Once they acquired horses, the Pawnee, Omaha, and other farming tribes began going on occasional buffalo hunts. But they still lived in settled villages and continued to grow most of their food. Other Indian peoples, such as the Cheyenne and Crow, gave up farming altogether and began a new way of life built around the buffalo. They were joined by different Indian groups, such as the Lakota (often called the Teton Sioux) and the Comanche, who left lands east and north of the Plains to hunt the great herds.

Although each Plains Indian group was a separate people with its own customs and beliefs, the buffalo-hunting tribes had many ways in common. All spent their lives traveling in small bands from hunting camp to hunting camp. Constantly on the move, they were very disciplined people led by men who had earned the respect of their band. To accommodate their mobile way of life, they developed the tepee—a comfortable cone-shaped dwelling made of buffalo skins placed over a wooden-pole frame. Tepees were light to carry and easy to put up and take down.

On horseback, a hunter could run alongside a stampeding buffalo and shoot arrows into its hide. To kill a large number of buffalo at once, Plains Indians also used the jump kill. Working together, mounted hunters rode toward a herd, yelling as loud as they could to scare the animals. When the buffalo started running, the men chased them, directing the herd off a nearby cliff. Skilled hunters could bring home as many as one hundred buffalo from a single jump kill.

Because their lives centered on the buffalo hunt, Plains Indians revered great hunters and warriors. Skilled

hunters gave their bands everything they needed to survive. The buffalo they killed provided the people with meat to eat, skins and furs to wear, and hides to cover their tepees. Brave warriors protected the band from enemies. They

In this painting, Crow Indian hunters armed with bows and arrows race into a buffalo herd.

The French in the West

By the late seventeenth century, another group of Europeans had arrived in the West—the French. In 1673–1674, French trader Louis Jolliet, accompanied by a priest named Jacques Marquette, explored the upper reaches of the Mississippi River. They were followed in 1682 by Robert Cavelier, Sieur de La Salle, who sailed the complete length of the river. Based on their explorations, France claimed the entire Mississippi Valley.

As the losers in the French and Indian War (1754–1763), the French were forced to forfeit most of their land claims in what is now the United States. Frenchmen, however, continued to do business at posts along the Mississippi, the most important of which was St. Louis. Most of the Frenchmen were traders, who made a living by offering Indians European goods in exchange for animal furs.

A Dakota Sioux woman, photographed in 1910, stretching and cleaning a buffalo hide

also helped tribes grow more powerful by pushing rival Indian groups off the best hunting grounds.

In Plains Indian cultures, hunters and warriors were almost always men. The work of women, though, was equally important. In addition to tending the band's horses, they were responsible for skinning the killed buffalo, drying the animals' meat, and tanning their hides. The work was difficult and time-consuming. If a hunter killed four or five buffalo in a few hours on the hunt, his wife might have to spend weeks turning his kill into products their people could use.

Even the best buffalo hunters sometimes had to rely on help from farming tribes. If a band could not find a herd or if bad weather ruined a hunt, they might not have enough buffalo meat

to feed themselves. They then had to trade with or steal from farming people to obtain food.

By the mid-eighteenth century, Plains Indians also traded with the occasional Spaniards or Frenchmen who came to their lands. From these Europeans, they obtained unfamiliar goods, such as guns and metal tools. These items proved so useful that the Indians quickly made them part of their way of life. Guns were better for hunting and warring than their own bows and arrows; metal tools were more durable than the ones they made themselves from rock and bone.

Dealing with these newcomers, though, had its dangers, as Sweet Medicine had warned the Cheyenne. He told them, "Some day you will meet a people who are white. They will try always to give you things, but do not take them. At last I think you will take these things that they offer you, and this will bring sickness to you."

Indeed, European diseases killed many Plains peoples. The farming Indians left on the Plains were particularly hard hit because, in the close quarters of their villages, the illnesses spread quickly. Even Indian tribes that did not encounter whites themselves were often infected by other Indians or animals.

As devastating as the European diseases were, they were only part of Sweet Medicine's dire prediction about what whites would bring to the Plains. "Your ways will change," he warned. "You will . . . forget good things by which you have lived and in the end become worse than crazy."

In fact, as non-Indians flocked to the Plains in the nineteenth century, the changes they brought would all but destroy the Plains Indian cultures.

The California Missions

In 1769 the Spanish officials in Mexico City became worried. They heard rumors that Russians were building posts along the coast of California on land claimed for the Spanish king and queen. The officials quickly sent an expedition, led by Gaspar de Portolá, to establish California settlements of their own and keep the Russians out. But the expedition member who would play the greatest role in California

French explorer Robert Cavelier, Sieur de La Salle, encountering Indians living along the Mississippi River. The painting, by George Catlin, was one of a series depicting La Salle's adventures commissioned by King Louis Philippe of France in the 1840s.

The San Gabriel Mission, as it appeared in 1832

Father Junípero Serra

history was a Catholic priest named Junípero Serra.

When he set out for California, Serra was fifty-six, in his day already an old man. His health was poor. He was so frail that two men had to hoist him onto his horse. Often he had to be carried on a stretcher. But Serra's goal was so important that nothing would stop him: He was determined to convert the Indians of California to Christianity. Like many Europeans, he had little understanding of or respect for the Indians' own religious beliefs. Serra was certain that without his instruction, the Indians would be damned to hell when they died. He wanted to save their souls so they could spend eternity in heaven with the Christian God.

Serra began his work by founding a mission—a complex of buildings including a church and living quarters for both the priests and their Indian converts—on the site of

the present-day city of San Diego. Before his death in 1784, Serra established eight other missions. The priests who continued his work built twelve more.

A few Indians—often survivors of epidemics of European diseases that had swept through villages—willingly came to live at the missions. In some California tribes, as many as nine out of ten people died when the epidemics hit. Often there were not enough villagers left even to bury the dead. With their villages destroyed and all their family and friends gone, the miserable survivors found food and shelter at the missions.

Most California Indians, however, were forced to move to the missions at gunpoint. Priests sent soldiers into the hills to round them up, and not having guns themselves, the Indians were unable to resist the armed men. Once at the mission, not only were the Indians taught about Christianity, but they were also put to work farming the mission's fields and tending the priests' livestock. The missions grew wealthy from Indian labor.

For the Indians, though, the living conditions at the missions were bleak and unhealthy. Indians were often given spoiled food and polluted water and crowded into small quarters, where germs spread quickly. In these unsanitary surroundings, many died of disease. During the 50-year period the missions were in operation, their Indian population dropped from 72,000 to 18,000.

The Indians also suffered under the hands of the priests, who beat any Indian who refused to follow their rules. In Serra's eyes, this treatment was justified because the Indians were like children and the priests were like parents. He thought his duty was to use discipline to guide the Indians toward what was true and right and even argued that the beatings were proof that "we, every one of us, came here for the single purpose of doing them good and for their eternal salvation."

Certainly, many of the Indians felt differently. Some became so worn down by their treatment at the missions that they ran away. A few runaways were taken in by nearby Indian villages and then joined in raids on the missions to steal food and supplies. Others were caught by soldiers the priests sent to find them. At the missions, runaways were whipped in public to teach the other Indians a lesson in obedience.

The California mission system ended only after Mexico won its independence from Spain in 1821. Gradually, some Indians were allowed to leave their missions to live as free people for the first time. Finally, in 1834, Mexico outlawed Indian slavery and all the mission Indians were freed. Many cheered as they emerged from the mission walls. Although the Mexican government was supposed to give the Indians about half of the lands owned by the missions, most of it passed into the hands of wealthy Mexicans instead. Some Indians stayed on, working as farmhands and ranch hands for small wages. Others turned away from non-Indians completely. Although their own villages had been destroyed, they found new homes with California Indian groups who had escaped the influence of the mission priests.

The Northwest Fur Trade

In 1778 two ships commanded by English explorer James Cook sailed up the northern Pacific Coast to what is now British Columbia, Canada. Docking their vessels in Nootka Sound, the explorers went ashore on present-day

The San Gabriel Rebellion

Although weakened by mission life, Indians often found the strength to revolt against Spanish rule. One of the largest mission rebellions occurred in 1785 at the San Gabriel Mission, near what is now Los Angeles. The revolt's leader was a medicine woman named Toypurina. Convinced that her powers would protect them, six villages of Indians joined her in an uprising against the San Gabriel priests. The Spaniards, however, had been warned of the attack in advance, and their well-prepared soldiers crushed the revolt and arrested Toypurina. Speaking on her own behalf at the trial, she accused the Spanish priests and military officials of driving Indians to rebellion by their harsh treatment. Perhaps swayed by her speech, the Spanish court chose not to execute her. Instead, she was exiled to the San Carlos Mission, where she could no longer influence her fellow San Gabriel rebels.

CHINOOK JARGON

Nootka, Americans, Chinook, English, Russians, Clatsop, French, and Spaniards—all these people participated in the Northwest fur trade. To make deals, they had to talk with one another, but each group had its own language. To solve the problem, they developed a special trade language called Chinook Jargon.

Chinook Jargon was easy to learn and easy to use. Within a few weeks, anyone could master it. The language used only about five hundred words. Most were Chinook in origin, but some came from English, French, and other Indian languages, such as Nootka and Salish. By combining these words to make new words and phrases, traders could make simple requests, demands, and offers. Although it could not communicate complicated information, Chinook Jargon gave traders of different backgrounds enough of a common tongue to do business with one another.

Examples of words in Chinook Jargon

mahkook man meant "merchant"
mahkook = purchase (Nootka)
man = man (English)

mitlite hiyu iktas pe dolla meant "rich"
mitlite = possess (Chinook)
hiyu = plenty (of) (Nootka)
iktas = goods (Chinook)
dolla = dollars (English)

mamook huy-huy meant "to trade"
mamook = make (Nootka)
huy-huy = (an) exchange (Jargon; mimics the sound of the French *oui, oui*, meaning "yes, yes")

A wooden bowl in the shape of a beaver was made by a Northwest Indian carver. Many Indians in the region traded beaver furs for European goods.

Vancouver Island. The English crew had assumed they were the first non-Indians to visit the area. But when they saw American Indians on the island using European tools, they realized they were not. The Indians had traded with non-Indians before, and eager to do so again, offered the Englishmen 1,500 sea otter furs in exchange for European goods. To the English, the trade seemed good. They were heading for China, and the weather was likely to turn cold before they arrived. The plush furs would be perfect material for the warm clothing they needed for their journey.

When they reached China, the English discovered that the furs were even more precious than they had thought. By selling just one fur, an English seaman could make the amount he normally earned in a year.

Cook described the sea otter trade in an account of his voyages that was published in 1784, five years after his death. Imagining the huge profits they could make, English and American traders rushed to the Pacific Coast. Their presence infuriated the Spanish colonials, who had claimed the lands for themselves. Indeed, a Spanish

expedition lead by Juan Pérez had sailed to British Columbia in 1774, four years before Cook. Spanish traders had made the first contact with these Indians. The competing claims to the northern Pacific Coast almost led to a war between England and Spain. But in the end, Spain decided trading rights in the area were not worth fighting for and in 1790 forfeited its rights in the area to the English.

Even though Spain was out of the picture, the English had plenty of other competitors. Russian traders, who had been dealing with Alaska natives for decades, began traveling south. Americans too were expanding their influence in the Pacific fur trade. In 1792 American explorer Robert Gray sailed up the Columbia, the river that now forms the boundary between Oregon and Washington. His exploration enabled the United States to make a claim to the region and, with it, the right to control trade with the Indians there.

At that time, the Columbia River Indians were pleased to have the American traders in their midst. Unlike the Spaniards, the Americans did not want to take over their land or destroy their religion. They just wanted their furs and were willing to pay good prices for them.

Tribes living at the mouth of the Columbia, such as the Chinook and Clatsop, became skilled negotiators. Knowing that the Americans could not afford to go home empty-handed, the Indians learned to demand top dollar for even poor-quality furs. Coastal Indians also made fortunes by traveling inland, buying furs cheaply from Indians there, and reselling them to American traders for a huge profit. The Northwest fur trade made these Indians wealthy, but the good times were not to last. As the nineteenth century began, more and more Americans started heading West— not just to trade, but to stay.

This engraving, made in the 1780s, shows the interior of a Nootka house. Racks used for drying salmon hang from the ceiling.

A mask made by the Haida Indians of British Columbia from copper, shell, and sea otter fur

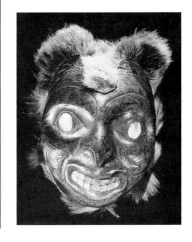

CHAPTER THREE

AMERICA HEADS WEST

1803 to 1847

In 1803 President Thomas Jefferson made perhaps the best real-estate deal in history. At the time, the United States stretched only from the Atlantic Ocean to the Mississippi River. The lands west of the Mississippi River to the Rocky Mountains, then called Louisiana, were claimed by France. Napoleon I, the dictator of France, had hoped to build a great empire there, but the project was just too expensive. Reluctantly, he offered to sell this territory to Jefferson for about $15 million.

West with Lewis and Clark

The deal was a bargain. The United States had been willing to pay close to that amount for the French-owned city of New Orleans alone. By buying Louisiana, in one stroke the president doubled the size of the United States.

Still, some people questioned the wisdom of the Louisiana Purchase. The price may have been low, but what had the United States actually bought? Few non-Indians had ever ventured into the region, so almost no Americans, not even the president, really knew what was there. So Jefferson sent an expedition, headed by Meriwether Lewis and William Clark, to journey west and report back on everything they encountered—from

◀ *Opposite page: Travelers heading west carve their initials at Independence Rock, Wyoming.*

Sacagawea and Jean-Baptiste

In 2000 the U.S. Mint issued a new gold-colored dollar coin bearing the images of two members of the Lewis and Clark Expedition—a Shoshone Indian woman named Sacagawea and her baby son, Jean-Baptiste Charbonneau.

Officially, Sacagawea was on hand as an interpreter. But equally important was her role as a peacekeeper. Her presence in the expedition party told the Indians that the explorers were not looking for a fight. Clark wrote, "The sight of this Indian woman [assures them] of our friendly intentions, as no woman ever accompanies a war party of Indians in their quarter."

Though just a baby, Jean-Baptiste made his own contribution to the expedition by helping keep up the crew's spirits. He grew up to become a great adventurer who spent his adult life wandering through the West as a fur trader, mountain man, army guide, and gold miner.

the rivers and lakes, to the plants and animals, to the Indian peoples. He also wanted the Lewis and Clark Expedition to search for a water route to the Pacific Ocean. Such a route would mean a good deal of money to American businessmen, who could use it to sail to Asia faster and easier than ever before.

Lewis and Clark approached their job very differently. Lewis was quiet and studious, always making detailed notes on whatever he saw. Friendly and outgoing, Clark was a little lazy about keeping his journal up-to-date, but he was well liked by their crew. Together they made an ideal team. Long after the expedition was over, they remained close friends.

In May 1804 the expedition started out from St. Louis, Clark's hometown. In addition to Lewis and Clark, about 50 men were in the party, including Clark's African-American slave, York. By boat, they headed up the Missouri River to the villages of the Mandan and Hidatsa Indians. There they spent the winter and met several Frenchmen who traded with the Indians. They hired one, Toussaint Charbonneau, along with his Shoshone Indian wife, Sacagawea, to join the expedition as interpreters.

By April the winter snows had thawed and the explorers were ready to continue. They loaded a boat with maps, records, Indians artifacts, and scientific specimens—including a live prairie dog—and sent a few men to take

Meriwether Lewis

William Clark

the items to the president to show him how much progress they were making. Lewis and Clark then gathered their 33-member crew into a fleet of canoes and headed out on the Missouri River. By the end of the month, they had reached present-day Montana. No other white person had ever traveled so far west along the Missouri.

At the beginning of June, the expedition faced a crisis when they came to a fork in the river. Most of the

"[W]e were now about to penetrate a country at least two thousand miles in width, on which the foot of civilized man had never trodden; . . . I could but esteem this moment of my departure as among the most happy of my life."

—explorer Meriwether Lewis, on the day the Lewis and Clark Expedition set off west on the Missouri River in April 1805

expedition members thought the Missouri was the branch to the north, but Lewis and Clark believed the branch to the south was the correct one. Although they did not agree with the explorers, the rest of the team followed Lewis and Clark's lead. To everyone's relief, they soon came to a great waterfall. The Hidatsa had told them that if they found a waterfall, they would know they were on course.

Assured that they were headed in the right direction, Lewis and Clark were confident they would soon find the water route to the Pacific. But their hopes were dashed on August 12, when Lewis climbed up Lemhi Pass along the border of present-day Montana and Idaho. Instead of a great river heading west, he saw only more and more mountains. To their deep disappointment, Lewis and Clark knew they would have to cross the Rockies on land.

They had no time to waste. Winter was coming, and if they did not start over the mountains quickly, they might be stranded in the Rockies when heavy snows began to fall. With no river to follow, their boats were worthless. The expedition needed horses. From the Hidatsa, Lewis and Clark had learned that the best horse traders in the area were the Shoshone, Sacagawea's people.

While riding ahead with a few men, Lewis encountered a young chief, whose name he soon discovered was Cameahwait. The explorer tried to communicate with Cameahwait through

A journal kept by William Clark

American painter Charles M. Russell's depiction of Sacagawea interpreting for Lewis and Clark on the Columbia River

sign language, but had little success. To his relief, the rest of the expedition quickly caught up with them. Lewis and Clark called a meeting with Cameahwait, with Sacagawea acting as an interpreter. While they spoke, Sacagawea looked oddly at the chief and then, in Lewis's words, "jumped up, ran & embraced him, & threw her blanket over him and cried profusely." She recognized him as her younger brother, whom she had not seen for several years. Delighted by the unexpected reunion, Cameahwait gave the expedition all the horses they needed. Nearly as important, the Shoshone also offered valuable advice about where best to cross the great mountains that stood between them and the ocean.

Even with the Indians' help, the trip over the Rockies proved brutal. Maneuvering through steep rock, the group ran short of food, and snow began to fall. Worse, as one expedition member wrote, "the mountains continue as far as our eyes could extend." After 11 days, the starving travelers finally made it across. Taken in by the Nez Percé Indians, many of the men made themselves sick as they hungrily devoured as much salmon as they could.

After making new canoes, the expedition set out again by water. They traveled down the Clearwater and Snake rivers to the great Columbia, which took them straight toward the ocean. In November Lewis and Clark finally reached the Pacific. Revealing their respect for the expedition members, the leaders held a vote to decide where they should spend the winter.

Included in the decision were Sacagawea and York—the first woman and African American permitted to vote on what would become American soil. The party elected to stay along the Columbia near what is now Astoria, Oregon, where the explorers built Fort Clatsop as their winter home.

Come spring, Lewis and Clark headed back east. Because they knew what to expect, the return trip proved far easier. On September 23, 1806, five months to the day since leaving Fort Clatsop, the expedition arrived in St. Louis. The residents cheered as they saw the explorers sailing down the Mississippi. They had been gone for more than two years, so most Americans had long since given them up for dead.

Lewis and Clark were given a hero's welcome. When they traveled to Washington, D.C., to report on their expedition, great parties and balls were staged in their honor. Yet despite the celebrations, the Lewis and Clark Expedition was in some ways a terrible failure. The explorers had not found a water route to the Pacific as Jefferson had hoped. Even worse, the trail they blazed was practically worthless for later travelers. The route was so dangerous that few people were willing to risk taking it.

The story of their adventure, though, made many Americans excited about the West. After Lewis's and Clark's journals were published, Louisiana no longer seemed like the great unknown. Now it was the home of mighty rivers, great forests, fertile lands, exotic wild plants and animals, and unfamiliar Indian peoples. Intrigued by what Lewis and Clark told them, many Americans wanted to learn more. The most adventurous set out to see the West for themselves.

Men of the Mountains

Soon after Lewis and Clark returned home, a young boy named Jedediah Smith read their journals and vowed that one day he too would explore the western wilderness. True to his dream, Smith grew up to be a mountain man—

One of the medals Lewis and Clark gave to Indians as a token of friendship

A trout drawn by William Clark on a page in his journal

Seaman

On the Lewis and Clark Expedition, Meriwether Lewis brought along his best friend—a big Newfoundland dog named Seaman. Lewis's pet soon proved his worth. He was good at catching beaver, whose tails made one of the crew's favorite meals. Once Seaman even hunted down an antelope, a wild animal several times his size. Lewis wrote that throughout the journey, the crew was safe from bear attacks because "our dog gives us timely notice of their visits, he keeps constantly patrolling all night." A Shawnee Indian who met the expedition offered Lewis three beaver skins for the talented dog, but Lewis refused, making it clear Seaman was not for sale at any price.

The Great Pathfinder

As the mountain men were exploring the West, the U.S. government sent out several expeditions of its own. The most famous was headed by John C. Frémont, an officer with the government's Corps of Topographical Engineers.

In 1842 Frémont's first expedition went from St. Louis across present-day southern Wyoming. With several mountain men as his guides, he followed a route pioneered by early western traders, which became known as the South Pass route of the Oregon Trail. Along the way, Frémont and his men studied the terrain and collected specimens of wild plants and animals.

Then, in 1843, Frémont and an expedition team set off once again to explore what are now Oregon and northern California. The government printed a report of his findings, which inspired thousands of settlers to head for Oregon and made Frémont a celebrity. Even though his guides did the trailblazing, he was nicknamed the Great Pathfinder.

John C. Frémont

An 1850 engraving showing a mountain man on the hunt

one of hundreds of animal trappers who roamed the West in the 1820s and 1830s.

By the early 1800s trading animal furs had long been a profitable business in the East. Beaver furs were particularly valuable. In Europe and the eastern United States, fashionable men and women dressed in coats trimmed with beaver fur. Wealthy men also wore felt hats made from the underside of beaver pelts.

After the Lewis and Clark Expedition, some fur trading companies decided to expand their operations west of the Mississippi. They hired mountain men

to trap beavers in this unfamiliar region. At first the trappers traveled by boat, but they soon had trouble on the Missouri River in Arikara Indian territory. In 1823 the Arikara attacked and killed 15 men working for William Ashley. As a result, Ashley decided his employees would be safer if they found an overland route west. Seeking easy travel routes and good hunting grounds, Ashley's trappers and those of other fur companies started exploring areas never seen by non-Indians. Jedediah Smith himself found South Pass, a valley in the Rockies where travelers could easily cross the great mountain range.

Most of the year, the mountain man's life was lonely and hard. Largely working by themselves, these adventurers had to travel over rough terrain, looking for riverbeds where they could set their traps. Often they had no food, and they always had to be on the lookout for danger. A careless mountain man might accidentally tumble from a cliff or become the prey of an angry grizzly bear.

Not surprisingly, mountain men looked forward to a break from their exhausting routine at an annual rendezvous. These monthlong get-togethers, held in late summer, attracted as many as one thousand trappers, traders, and Indians. At the rendezvous, mountain men met up with traders, who bought their furs and gave them the supplies they needed for the next year. The rendezvous was not just a business meeting, though. It was also a wild party where mountain men sang, danced, drank, and gambled with one another. Some got so caught up in the festivities that they frittered away all their earnings for the past year.

The mountain man's way of life did not last long. By about 1840 most were out of jobs because, over the years, they had caught so many beavers that there were few left to trap. In addition, the wealthy were tired of beaver hats and trim. Beaver pelts no longer brought high prices, so fur companies stopped paying mountain men to hunt for them.

However brief, the era of the mountain men changed the United States forever. By finding routes through the West, the mountain men helped continue the work Lewis and Clark had started. Hearing stories of their journeys, Americans learned that the West was not a barren wilderness. Some areas—especially places west of the Rockies—offered rich, fertile land that American farmers began to want for their own. And thanks to the pioneering mountain men, known trails could now take them there.

A beaver hat

This illustration depicts a legendary encounter trapper S. E. Hollister had with a mother bear protecting her cubs.

GEORGE CATLIN, INDIAN PAINTER

While still in his twenties, a young Philadelphia artist named George Catlin saw a delegation of Plains Indians traveling through the city on its way to meet with the president in Washington, D.C. Thrilled by their exotic looks and clothing, Catlin made a promise to himself: One day, he would "[visit] their country, and [become] their historian."

Several years later, in 1830, Catlin traveled to St. Louis and became the friend of explorer William Clark. By 1832 he had set off on the first of many trips to the lands of western Indians. With a trader as an interpreter, he introduced himself to the tribes he met; then, once the Indians knew he was friendly, he brought out his paints and pencils and began depicting what he saw. Although other non-Indian artists had painted western Indians, Catlin was the first to visit their homelands in an effort to create an accurate visual record of their way of life.

The Indians of the West were nearly as fascinated with Catlin as he was with them. Before meeting him, they had never seen a realistic portrait. They painted their own pictures using vegetable dyes and leaves, but these materials could not produce the highly detailed works Catlin could create with commercial paints and brushes.

George Catlin painting Mandan leader Mah-to-toh-pa while his tribespeople look on

He wrote of the Mandan Indians' stunned reaction to his paintings: "[M]any of the gaping multitude commenced yelping; some were stamping off in the jarring dance . . . hundreds covered their mouths."

From 1832 to 1840, Catlin made more than five hundred paintings of Indians. He spent many more years traveling throughout the United States and Europe with Catlin's Indian Gallery. This touring exhibition featured his paintings and displays of some eight tons of Indian clothing and artifacts he had collected during his travels.

The Trail of Tears

Not all people living east of the Mississippi River were eager to travel west. Among them were the Indians who made their homes in the lands between the Appalachian Mountains and the Mississippi. These Indian nations had occupied their territories for centuries and had no desire to leave the lands of their ancestors.

American settlers, though, had other ideas. They wanted the Indians' land, much of which was rich and good for farming. Even though they had no right to the land, many settlers began moving into tribal territories. Angry at the newcomers, Indians tried several times to drive them away. Beginning in 1805 the Shawnee brothers Tecumseh and Tenskwatawa worked to unite the tribes to fight invading settlers, but they were defeated by American troops. Their movement fell into disarray after Tecumseh's death in battle in 1813.

A similar fate met the attempt of Sauk and Fox leader Black Hawk to hold on to his homeland. A few Sauk and Fox chiefs signed a treaty with the U.S. government, agreeing to leave present-day Illinois and move across the Mississippi. But in 1832 Black Hawk and two thousand followers refused to follow the treaty terms, and war broke out. The U.S. soldiers battled Black Hawk's people, slaughtering many men, women, and children. Their bloody defeat convinced other midwestern tribes that there was little point in resisting American forces determined to relocate them.

The U.S. Congress also tried to force Indians west by passing the Indian Removal Act of 1830. This law allowed the president to negotiate with eastern tribes for their relocation, or removal, whether or not the Indians wanted to move. The main targets for removal were five large tribes in the Southeast— the Cherokee, Choctaw, Chickasaw, Creek, and Seminole. During the 1830s these peoples were forced to leave their homes and journey hundreds of miles to Indian Territory (now Oklahoma).

All the tribes suffered greatly, but the Cherokee's removal was perhaps the worst of all. Americans who believed white ways and Indian ways were just too different supported removal because

A portrait of Black Hawk by George Catlin

The Seminole of Florida went to war with the United States to fight their removal to Indian Territory. They were led by a great warrior, Osceola. At a treaty council in 1823, he was asked to sign a document that called for the Seminole to surrender their homeland. He refused, and instead plunged his knife into the treaty to show that he would never leave without a fight.

The resulting conflict— the Second Seminole War (1835–1842)—was one of the longest and most expensive wars in all of U.S. history. Although most of the Seminole eventually moved to Indian Territory, about five hundred hiding in Florida's dense swamplands could not be forced out. Rather than continue the costly conflict, the United States admitted defeat and allowed them to stay. Their descendants still live in southern Florida.

The Trail of Tears, *painted by Robert Lindneux in 1942*

Cherokee leader Sequoyah, *with the Cherokee alphabet*

they thought whites could not share lands with Indians. The Cherokee, however, had almost all the same customs as their white neighbors. Most were settled farmers. They attended Christian churches and established excellent schools. They had written laws and a government modeled after that of the United States. Still, land-hungry whites claimed the Cherokee were too "uncivilized" to live among them.

The Cherokee's leaders did everything they could to block removal, including taking two lawsuits to the U.S. Supreme Court. One challenged the state of Georgia, which was trying to destroy the Cherokee government. Although the Court ruled in the Cherokee's favor, President Andrew Jackson sympathized with the Georgians and made no effort to enforce the ruling.

In 1837, after years of fighting removal, the Cherokee Nation was invaded by armed soldiers who herded the Cherokee into dirty camps and destroyed and looted their homes. Then, with little more than the clothes on their backs, the Cherokee were forced at gunpoint to march to Indian Territory. The journey was miserable. The U.S. government was supposed to provide the Indians with food and supplies, but officials stole much of what was bought for them. With little to eat, some Cherokee starved, while many more became ill. By the time they reached Indian Territory, their path was littered with bodies. About four thousand people—one out of every four Cherokee who made the journey—died along the way. The Cherokee called their horrible trek west "the trail on which we cried." It is now known as the Trail of Tears.

The Cherokee's hard times were far from over. They now had to rebuild their nation from scratch. They had to learn how to farm in the dry, dusty soil of Indian Territory, which was far poorer than the farmland they had left behind. They had to build new schools and churches and establish a new government. Even more difficult, they had to mend rifts that removal had opened among their own people. Many Cherokee were furious at a few leaders who, feeling they had little choice, had helped the U.S. government force the Cherokee west. The resentment was so strong that in 1839 a group of vigilantes assassinated these leaders, an event that nearly plunged the tribe into civil war.

Traveling on the Oregon Trail

For white Americans in the East and Midwest, though, the West was beginning to seem like a wonderland. People were especially fascinated by tales of the Far West beyond the Rockies. The Gays of Springfield, Missouri, were just one family that became convinced that a better life awaited them there. "We had lived in Springfield three years and were very happy and prosperous and the future looked bright," Martha Gay Masterson wrote of her youth. Even so, in 1851, when Martha was thirteen, her father "got the Western fever. He talked about Oregon and the Columbia River . . . and wanted to go there."

By this time, many other Americans had also caught the "Western fever," which began spreading after the first group of settlers traveled overland to Oregon and California in 1841. News of what they had found there made many more want to follow. Both areas boasted a mild climate and plenty of rich farmland and hunting grounds. According to one tall tale, fully cooked wild pigs stuck with forks roamed the Oregon countryside, just waiting for hungry travelers to grab them.

Traveling to Oregon from Missouri took about six months. Most travelers—known as overlanders—made their way on foot, covering about 15 miles a day. Only the very young and the very old rode in great wagons that carried their supplies. So that they could help one another along the way, several families usually traveled together in trains of 20 or more wagons.

The Donner Party

"Our ignorance of the route was complete," wrote John Bidwell, who traveled on the first wagon train to California in 1841. Later overlanders had an advantage over these early travelers. They could purchase guidebooks that told them the best routes west.

Even following a guidebook was not without its hazards. On the advice of the popular *Emigrants' Guidebook to Oregon and California*, 89 members of the 1846 Donner party took a shortcut through the rugged Sierra Nevada on the way to California. The decision led to disaster. Winter snowstorms left the group trapped in the mountains. Facing starvation, several party members had to eat the flesh of those who had died. Only half survived to tell the horrible tale of their ordeal.

The Donner Party, struggling to make its way through the snow-covered Sierra Nevada

The Trails West

Though the most heavily traveled, the Oregon Trail was only one of several routes west. Here are some other popular trails:

THE SANTA FE TRAIL: In the early 1820s this trail was developed as a trade route between Missouri settlements and the then-Mexican town of Santa Fe. Thousands of miners also followed this path west.

THE CALIFORNIA TRAIL: First blazed in 1841, this route was an offshoot of the Oregon Trail that took travelers to what is now Sacramento, California. It was a popular trail for pioneers until the Donner Party tragedy of 1846.

THE MORMON TRAIL: Traveling from Nauvoo, Illinois, to Salt Lake City, in present-day Utah, the Mormons pioneered this new route along the north bank of the Platte River in 1847.

THE BOZEMAN TRAIL: Mapped out by John M. Bozeman between 1863 and 1865, this trail offered miners the most easily traveled route to goldfields near Virginia City in present-day Montana.

Martha was not happy about leaving her friends. But as she later wrote, "children were expected to do as their parents said in those days and father said we must come." For months the Gays planned their trip. Her father sold their house and furniture while her mother sewed clothing for the journey. The family bought four wagons and enough supplies "to stock a small grocery store." Finally, in April 1851, they set out, the streets of Springfield crowded with friends who gathered to see them off.

The Gays traveled on the Oregon Trail, a path that was well worn: Between 1840 and 1860 about 250,000 people followed it west. The route first took them over the flatlands now called the Great Plains; it then led them through South Pass, over the Rockies, and down the raging Cascade River into Oregon. Americans who traveled the Oregon Trail were leaving not only their homes, but also their country, because much of the land they crossed then belonged to Mexico. Oregon was claimed by both the United States and England.

Soon Martha learned firsthand about the many dangers of the journey. She was frightened of drowning when they had to cross deep rivers. "How we

trembled as we watched the long train starting in," she wrote about crossing the South Platte River, whose waters rose high after the spring rains. Martha also feared being trampled by stampeding buffalo herds. She remembered that "the earth trembled under their weight." Even her fellow travelers could be a threat. A disagreement over how fast to travel was settled only after "one man drew his gun to shoot another."

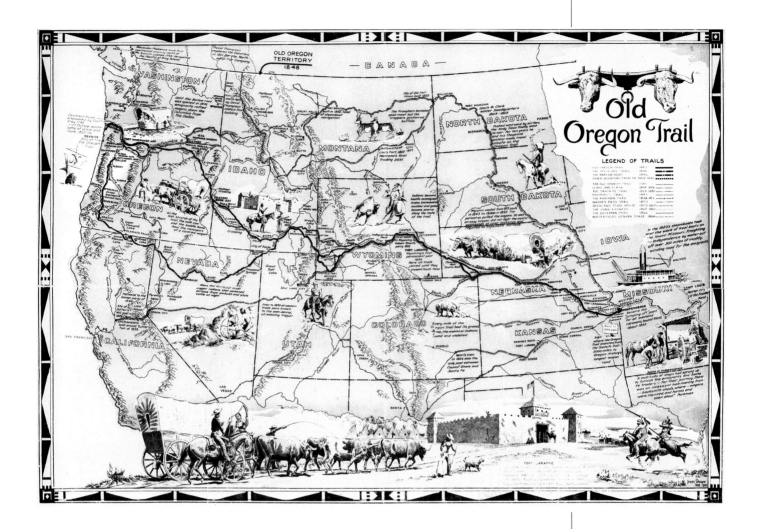

Because their parents were preoccupied with keeping the wagon train moving, the children were often left to look after themselves, sometimes with near fatal results. Martha watched a two-year-old boy fall under a wagon wheel and helped save a three-year-old girl from tumbling over a two-hundred-foot cliff. She and her young friends became accustomed to seeing children's graves along the trail.

Martha also worried constantly about Indian attacks. Like most children of her day, she had been taught to think

A map issued in 1918, commemorating the Oregon Trail

An 1849 drawing of a wagon train crossing the Platte River

African Americans in Texas

With the flood of Americans into Mexican Texas came more than five thousand African Americans. Most were slaves. Slavery was illegal in Mexico, so to appease Mexican authorities, Texan slave owners called their slaves "contract laborers." But the change in name meant little. The contract laborers were still slaves, forced to do whatever their owners demanded.

A small number of free African Americans also chose to settle in Texas, where they hoped to find better treatment in Mexico than they could in the American South. Many prospered as farmers, tradesmen, and merchants. Among them was William Goyens, who became one of the wealthiest men in the region.

Warring with Mexico

In the 1830s deserted cabins all over the states of Alabama, Mississippi, and Louisiana had notes reading "GTT" tacked to their doors. Everyone who passed knew exactly what the letters meant. The family who used to live there had Gone To Texas.

While easterners and midwesterners headed to Oregon and California for land, southerners more often went to Texas, which was then part of Mexico. Stephen Austin was one of the first Americans to settle there. When he arrived in 1821, only a few Mexican planters, known as Tejanos, lived in Texas. The Mexican government worried that the United States would try to take over the area if it remained unsettled. But Mexico could not persuade its own citizens to move north into Texas, so it allowed Austin to take hundreds of American families south to settle there. The Americans, called Texans (or *Texians* until the

Republic of Texas was established in 1836), pledged loyalty to Mexico in exchange for rich farmland. Their farms cost them only 12½ cents an acre—one tenth the price of similar land in the United States.

The Mexican scheme to settle Texas worked. By 1835 more than 30,000 Texans lived there, outnumbering the Tejanos nearly ten to one. But the Mexican

Santa Anna

"It is not uncommon for ladies to mount their mustangs and hunt with their husbands, and with them to camp out for days on their excursions to the sea shore for fish and oysters. All visiting is done on horseback, and they will go fifty miles to a ball with their silk dresses, made perhaps in Philadelphia or New Orleans, in their saddlebags."

—*Texan settler Mary Austin Holley, on the ways of American women in Texas*

government was far from happy with the situation. Some Texans, who considered themselves more American than Mexican, began saying they should fight Mexico for their independence. They made their first move at the Mexican army post at Gonzales in 1835. There, Mexican soldiers told the Texans to surrender a cannon. The Texans replied by pointing the cannon at the Mexicans and flying a homemade flag that said "Come and Get It."

As more Mexican troops were sent into Texas, warfare broke out. By mid-December, the small Texan army had taken over the Mexican town of San Antonio. About 180 men held the town, holing up in an abandoned building known as the Alamo. To avenge the fall of San Antonio, Mexican dictator Antonio López de Santa Anna led a force of more than one thousand soldiers against the Texans. Even though the Alamo's defenders were

woefully outnumbered, they refused to surrender. On March 6, 1836, the Mexicans stormed the Alamo and killed all the Texans inside. Later that month, about 350 more Texan troops were executed at the post of Goliad.

As the Mexican army advanced, the Texan army, led by Sam Houston, made a hasty retreat. His own men begged him to turn and fight, but Houston refused. Santa Anna had too many soldiers. Houston knew he could beat Santa Anna only if the Mexicans made a mistake, and on April 21, 1836, at the San Jacinto River, Houston got his wish.

Sure he would defeat the Texans, Santa Anna sent half of his soldiers off on another campaign. The others he allowed to camp by the river, napping the afternoon away with only a few guards on duty. The Texans sneaked up on the sleeping soldiers. Shouting "Remember the Alamo" and "Remember Goliad," they made a surprise attack. In only 20 minutes the Texans won the battle and declared themselves free of Mexico. The victory spelled doom for the Tejanos. Even though many had

Sam Houston

Civil Disobedience

One American who felt the Mexican-American War was wrong was writer Henry David Thoreau. An opponent of slavery, he believed the war was just an excuse to take Mexican land and turn it into more American states where slavery would be legal. On moral grounds, Thoreau refused to pay a tax to support the war and spent a night in jail. He wrote of his experience in an essay, "Civil Disobedience." It argued that Americans should protest unfair laws by breaking them, as long as they were willing to accept punishment for their unlawful behavior. Thoreau's words would later inspire Martin Luther King, Jr., a leader in the fight for African-American civil rights in the 1960s.

Manifest Destiny

"Away, away with all these cobweb tissues of rights of discovery, exploration, settlement," wrote journalist John O'Sullivan. In an 1845 article for the *New York Morning News*, he argued that Americans had every right to settle in western lands all the way to the Pacific Ocean. To O'Sullivan, it mattered little that Mexico and England claimed much of this land or that Indian nations had lived there for centuries. He believed that it was the United States' "manifest destiny to overspread and to possess the whole of the continent," adding that God Himself wanted the country to expand westward. O'Sullivan's ideas appealed to many Americans, and his phrase "Manifest Destiny" became a rallying cry for politicians who wanted control of western land.

Davy Crockett became a folk hero for fighting Mexican troops at the Alamo.

fought on the Texans' side, the Texans drove the Tejanos from their homes to rid Texas of all Mexicans—friends as well as enemies.

At first, the Texans' lands became the Republic of Texas. But most Texans did not want an independent country; they wanted to be part of the United States. After some political wrangling, Texas became the twenty-eighth state on December 29, 1845. Texas statehood was a pet cause of the new president, James K. Polk. Making good on a campaign promise, he also negotiated with England to take control of lands in

present-day Oregon and Washington. Polk then set his sights on California, which was still part of Mexico. He tried to buy it, but the Mexican government refused even to consider selling it. If the president wanted to gain control of California, he would have to go to war.

To provoke a fight, Polk sent American troops to the Nueces River in Texas, which Mexico still considered Mexican territory. When Mexican soldiers shot at the troops, Polk declared that Mexico had launched a war against the United States. Although some Americans blamed Polk, not

Mexico, for starting the fighting, most supported the president.

Polk had no trouble recruiting army volunteers for the Mexican-American War. More than 73,000 young men signed up to fight. In their hometowns, they were honored during war rallies. Their mothers and wives sewed brilliant uniforms and flags for them to carry into battle. For most volunteers, though, the army experience hardly lived up to their grand send-off. Instead of the great adventure they had imagined, army life proved dirty, bleak, and boring. As one disappointed recruit wrote home, "Soldiering ain't what it is cracked up to be. . . . Glory & all that is nothing but Fudge."

Once the army was ready, the president planned a three-part campaign. Troops led by Zachary Taylor traveled south into Mexico and quickly won a series of battles. In the meantime, a second group of soldiers headed by Stephen Kearny marched overland into Santa Fe, then an important Mexican trading center. A third corps of troops moved toward northern California by ship. When they reached the coast, they found that American settlers there were already revolting against Mexican rule.

Although the war was going well for the United States, Mexico still refused to surrender. Polk decided to force the Mexicans to admit defeat by sending soldiers to Mexico City. In September 1847 American forces reached and captured the Mexican capital. The war was over.

Five months passed before Mexico and the United States agreed on the terms of the peace. In the 1848 Treaty of Guadalupe Hidalgo, Mexico was forced to give up not only California, but also lands in present-day New Mexico, Arizona, Nevada, Colorado, and Utah. In exchange, the United States paid Mexico a mere $15 million. President Polk's war, just or not, had achieved its goal: The United States now stretched from the Atlantic Ocean to the Pacific Ocean. His greatest prize—the lush lands of California—would soon prove more valuable than even Polk had imagined.

The Purchase of Alaska

The spirit of Manifest Destiny did not end quickly. Two decades after the United States extended its borders from ocean to ocean, the country acquired even more western territory in the area known as Alaska. This land had been claimed by Russia, but the Russian government could see little reason to spend the money needed to maintain a presence there. When Russia offered to sell Alaska, U.S. Secretary of State William Seward eagerly arranged to buy it for $7 million in 1867.

Many Americans thought Seward had made a foolish mistake and nicknamed his decision "Seward's Folly." Journalists joked that the government would have to appoint a superintendent of walruses and that the only product frigid Alaska had to offer was ice. In fact, the land proved rich in natural resources, particularly oil. Covering an area twice the size of Texas, Alaska cost the United States only two cents an acre.

Americans and Mexicans in battle during the Mexican-American War

CHAPTER FOUR

A LAND OF RICHES

1848 to 1860

O n the morning of January 24, 1848, James Marshall was up early, surveying the work done by his crew. He was supervising a group of laborers building a sawmill along the American River in northern California. Glancing at the stream, he saw something shiny. Marshall picked up the object, no bigger than a pea, and took a closer look. He later remembered that "it made my heart thump, for I was certain it was gold." Turning his eyes back to the water, Marshall saw more glistening specks. "Boys, I believe I have found a gold mine," he announced to his men.

The Rush to California

M arshall worked for John Sutter, who had come to Mexican California in 1834. An unsuccessful Swiss businessman, he hoped that there at last he would find his fortune. The smooth-talking Sutter had persuaded California's governor to give him a huge tract in the Sacramento Valley—50,000 acres of rich land—where he cleared fields, planted orchards, and built a fort. The work was done by Indian laborers he recruited from the Miwok and Nisenan tribes. When he did not find

◀ Opposite page: A crew of miners panning for gold during the California Gold Rush

This illustration mocks easterners hoping to become California miners. Wearing formal clothing and overloaded with mining equipment, the man seems unlikely to be successful in the rough-and-tumble atmosphere of the gold rush.

enough volunteers, Sutter thought nothing of forcing Indians to work for him at gunpoint.

Four days after his discovery at Sutter's Mill, Marshall returned to the fort to show his boss the shiny rocks he had found. Together they consulted an encyclopedia to make certain the rocks were really gold. Their tests showed the gold was 23-carat, almost pure. Sutter swore Marshall and his other workers to secrecy because he wanted to clear a solid legal claim to the land where Marshall had made his discovery before anyone else found out about the gold.

As Sutter began trying to buy the land from the Nisenan, his men stopped working on the mill and began searching

for their own stash of the precious metal. Slowly, rumors about the gold leaked out. One man who heard the news was Sam Brannan, who began building a store next to Sutter's Fort with all the equipment a miner would need. To make sure he had customers, Brannan then rode through the nearby town of San Francisco on May 12, 1848. "Gold! Gold! Gold from the American River!" he shouted out in the streets. Within days, San Francisco was nearly empty. Everyone who could rushed to Sutter's Fort with dreams of striking it rich.

The word spread quickly. Within one month, it reached Hawaii. Within two, the news made its way to Oregon. By the fall, miners from Mexico, Peru, and Chile were packing up and heading north to California.

In the meantime, wild stories were traveling through the East. One said that there was so much gold dust in the air that a California man found sixteen

Western Voices

"One day a miner gave me and the other children permission to dig on his claim. Diligently we set out to work, and carefully scooped up the soft dirt and then washed it, just as we had seen the men do many times. I was the luckiest one of the group and found a nugget worth five dollars. With this I bought a new pair of shoes of which I was sorely in need."

—*Martha Gentry, on digging for California gold when she was eleven years old*

THE WAY THEY GO TO CALIFORNIA.

This cartoon pokes fun at the forty-niners' desperation to reach California. Would-be miners are shown traveling by airship, parachute, and even rocket.

The Aerial Locomotive

In 1849 inventor Rufus Porter made an announcement that thrilled easterners frantic to reach California. The founder of *Scientific American* magazine, Porter designed what he called an aerial locomotive, a giant balloon that moved forward with steam engines. His passenger balloon, Porter claimed, could travel through the air as fast as one hundred miles an hour. According to his calculations, it could make a round-trip from New York to California in only seven days—a journey that would take about a year on a wagon train. Porter signed up some two hundred hopeful travelers at $50 a head before it became clear the inventor had overestimated his engineering know-how. Unable to build a "locomotive" that could actually fly, Porter could not get either his ambitious business or his airship off the ground.

dollars' worth just by washing out his beard. To determine what was happening in California, President James K. Polk sent an army expedition there. Headed by Lieutenant William Tecumseh Sherman, the force reported that the rumors about gold were not exaggerated. To drive their point home, the expedition members brought the president a container of four thousand dollars' worth of gold dust. Polk put it on display in Washington, D.C., for the public to see and in December 1848 he told the entire nation about the expedition's findings. Speaking to Congress, he declared that "the accounts of the abundance of gold in [California] are of such extraordinary character" that they challenged the imagination.

With the gold strike confirmed by the president himself, people throughout the East caught "gold fever." As the new year approached, thousands made plans to head for California. Leaving their homes for the western goldfields in 1849, they were nicknamed the forty-niners.

The forty-niners knew that if they wanted their share of the gold, they needed to get to California fast. There were two ways of making the trip: by land or by sea. Traveling overland along the well-worn wagon trails was cheaper, but it meant a long delay. The trip took about six months, and gold-seekers could not begin traveling until April, when the winter snows finally melted. Many who could afford the fare decided to go by ship. A popular water route took forty-niners from New York all the way around South America and north to San Francisco. One ship made the voyage in only 89 days.

Levi's Fortune

Many people who struck it rich during the gold rush were not miners, but merchants who made their fortunes by selling goods and services to the forty-niners. One of the most successful was a young New Yorker named Levi Strauss, who arrived in San Francisco in 1849. He brought with him a large supply of canvas cloth that he had intended to use to make tents. But once in California he saw that miners had a more pressing need—comfortable, durable work pants. Strauss's canvas pants became the miners' favorite work wear. He had even greater success when he later replaced the canvas with heavyweight blue denim and reinforced the pants with copper rivets. Strauss's new design was the first blue jeans, now the most popular style of pants in the world.

A mining camp on the Sacramento River

Either way, the trip was hard. On ships, travelers suffered from horrible seasickness. The little food they had was often full of worms and insects. On wagons, gold-seekers had to endure the same discomforts overlanders had faced since the early 1840s. In addition, they now had to deal with overcrowded trails full of easterners racing west, hoping to get there before the gold ran out. The smell of rotting oxen, driven so hard they fell dead, filled the air. Overeager gold-seekers tried taking shortcuts, only to find the alternate trails were more dangerous and sometimes even longer. A man named William Swain was so worn down by overland travel that he wrote his brother, begging him not to follow his example: "There was some talk between us of your coming to this country. For God's sake think not of it. Stay at home. Tell all who you know that are thinking of coming that . . . thousands have laid and will lay their bones along the routes to and in this country."

Life on Gold Mountain

When they finally reached California, the forty-niners found that earlier miners had already pocketed much of the loose gold. In the first months of the California Gold Rush, gold had been so easy to find that even children were successful. "My little girls can make from 5 to 25 dollars a day," boasted one man in a letter home. By late 1849 there was still gold to be mined, but now plenty of hard work and luck were needed to find it.

The forty-niners carried the simple tools of their trade: shovel, pick, and pan. They used shovels and picks to dig out chunks of rock, and pans to separate the gold from gravel and dirt. The work was backbreaking and nearly always unrewarding.

Gold miners with little money for equipment looked for gold using a

A group of American and Chinese miners at Auburn Ravine, California

method called panning. Taking a metal pan about the size of a dinner plate, they first dug up a scoop of sand from the bottom of a stream. The miners then carefully let water run over the pan, carrying the sand away with it. Because gold is heavier than sand, any gold mixed in sank to the bottom. If they were lucky, miners were left with a few tiny chunks of gold. More often, though, their work brought them little more than an empty pan.

Even if he did strike gold, a miner often had to spend his find for supplies in the towns that had grown up almost overnight near the mining camps. The towns had restaurants, laundries, and stores—all charging high prices. A single

egg cost about 50 cents (some ten dollars in today's money). Many miners' fortunes were also squandered in saloons and gambling houses. Sacramento alone boasted more than 40 gambling parlors, all intent on separating drunken, homesick miners from their gold.

Nearly all the forty-niners were young men who had left their wives and children back home. Still, a few women braved the rough male world of the mining camps and towns. One was Luzena Wilson, who later wrote, "I would not be left behind. I thought where [my husband] could go, I could, and where I went I could take my two little toddling babies." While cooking for her family at a camp in Nevada City,

> "Oh, the Good time has come at last.
> We need no more complain, Sir.
> The rich can live in luxury
> And the poor can do the same, Sir.
> For the Good time has come at last,
> and as we all are told, Sir.
> We shall be rich at once now
> With California Gold, Sir."
>
> *— popular song sung by the California forty-niners*

A San Francisco saloon and gambling parlor in 1855

Wilson was offered five dollars for a biscuit from a miner desperate for a home-cooked meal. Seeing a chance to make her own fortune, she set up a boardinghouse, which soon brought in far more money than her husband's gold-digging.

About two thirds of the forty-niners were Americans, mostly from the East and Midwest. Many were young veterans of the Mexican-American War who were eager for a new adventure. Others were ordinary farmers and laborers, who saw the gold rush as their one chance to better the lot of their families. One woman in Baltimore wrote her mother about her husband's decision to head to California: "Joseph has borrowed money to go. But I am full of bright visions that never before filled my mind . . . .[A]t the best of times I have never thought of much beyond a living, but now I am confident of being well off."

The rest of the forty-niners came from countries all over the globe. The mine fields were full of French, Germans, Irish, Russians, Italians, and Australians who believed a few months spent mining in California would earn them

Western Voices

"The present of this city is under canvas and the future on paper. Everything is new except the ground and trees and stars beneath which we sleep. Quarreling and cheating form the employments, drinking and gambling the amusements, making the largest pile of gold the only ambition of the inhabitants."

—*New York clergyman Daniel B. Woods, on the mining town of Sacramento in 1849*

more money than years of labor in their own lands. As foreigners flooded into San Francisco, the city housed people from more different cultures than anywhere else in the world.

Despite their varied pasts, white miners from the United States and Europe largely got along with one another. Those from other regions, though, were often abused. Although Mexicans, Chileans, and Peruvians were among the first and best miners to go to California, they were regularly harassed by American newcomers who considered these men their inferiors. Many Americans were also envious of the skills Mexicans and South Americans had acquired working mines in their own lands. Soon

after California became a state in 1850, its government passed a law that taxed all non-American miners $20 a month. The tax was so steep that many miners from Mexico and South America had to give up and go home.

Despite the tax, Chinese miners—who were mostly poor farmers from southern China—remained. They called California *Gam Saan*, or "Gold Mountain," in their language. To get there, these men had to borrow money from Chinese companies. One lured workers to Gam Saan with promises of "great pay, large houses, and food and clothing of the finest description." Yet by the time many Chinese men had reached California, they were so deep in debt that they had

Many Chinese worked as miners.

THE LEGEND OF JOAQUIN MURIETA

JOAQUIN MURIETA
by YELLOW BIRD (John Rollin Ridge)

I am Joaquin! Kill me if you can!" cried the hero of *The Life and Adventures of Joaquin Murieta, the Celebrated California Bandit.* The popular novel, written by Cherokee author John Rollin Ridge in 1854, told a story familiar to all Californians. In Ridge's tale, Murieta was a Mexican bandit, driven to crime after Americans whipped him and terrorized his family. A Robin Hood figure, Murieta got his revenge by robbing rich Americans and giving the spoils to California's poor Mexicans.

There may have been a real Joaquin Murieta, though no one knows for sure. California newspapers, however, told of a bandit with that name, whom California Mexicans celebrated for resisting abuse from white miners. Lawmen from Texas were called in to hunt the renegade, and in 1853 they killed a Mexican man they claimed was Murieta. The victim's head was placed in a jar and exhibited to the public in Sacramento. Despite the grisly evidence, many Mexicans claimed the wrong man had been killed. They believed Murieta lived to fight more battles against their enemies.

PICTURING THE WEST

In their makeshift camps, gold-rush miners lived in a rough world, far removed from the polite society they had left behind in the East. The colorful names they often gave their camps, such as Rough and Ready, Angel's Camp, Murderer's Bar, Mad Mule Gulch, and Sweet Revenge, reflected the life they lived—a wild existence full of gambling, violence, greed, and disappointment. Perhaps out of wishful thinking, the men at the Colorado mine pictured below chose an unusually genteel name for their camp— "Ocean Grove."

to continue mining no matter what. Living in their own camps isolated from other miners, the hardworking Chinese miners soon acquired a reputation for finding gold in areas Americans considered "played out"—empty or not worth the work. Their success made white miners resentful. Whites frequently attacked the Chinese, often cutting off the long braids, called queues, they wore down their backs, to humiliate them.

The worst treatment was reserved for Indians, who had initially joined the gold rush both as miners and traders offering necessary goods to the men flooding into California. But soon the forty-niners—without a thought—took over the land where the Indians gathered the plants and hunted the wild animals they needed to survive. Their territory lost, many Indians were left to starve. Others died of diseases the forty-niners brought with them from the East. Still others, including women and children, were brutally murdered by miners determined to rid the area of Indians once and for all.

The surviving Indians faced more threats from the California government. Although slavery was illegal in the state, the legislature passed a law that allowed the labor of Indians to be sold to the highest bidder. Whites kidnapped Indian children and set them to work in the mines or sold them as slaves. "Indians seven or eight years old are worth $100," one Californian wrote in passing. The victims of slaughter, slavery, disease, and starvation, the Indian tribes of

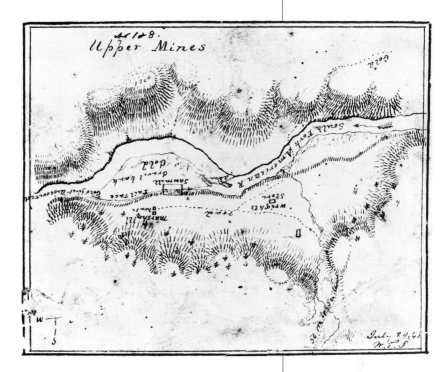

A map of Sutter's Mill

California were nearly destroyed during the gold rush era. In 1848 there were some 150,000 California Indians. In 1870 only 30,000 remained.

Despite the brutal measures white miners took to destroy their competition, the dream of striking it rich disappeared quickly. By about 1853 it was nearly impossible to find any gold through

Several decades after the California Gold Rush, a Colorado miner sets off with two mules loaded with supplies.

Wherever gold was discovered, boomtowns, like this one in Colorado, grew up nearby.

panning. What was left was buried deep within rock, and getting it out required firing at a rock face with a jet of water under such high pressure that "wherever it struck it tore away earth, gravel and boulders," as one witness observed. The equipment was expensive, so only large companies could afford it. Unable to find any gold on their own, some miners took jobs with these firms. When the companies found gold deposits, the already wealthy owners pocketed the profits. Their employees took home only a small wage.

Many disappointed miners returned home with nothing but stories of their adventure out west. Others stayed on and built new lives in California. These people helped make San Francisco first into a boomtown, then into a great city. In just four years after the discovery of gold at Sutter's Mill, San Francisco was transformed from a village of 900 to a bustling urban center of more than 36,000.

Some forty-niners were never quite able to get the thrill of the gold rush out of their blood. Whenever they heard rumors of a new gold or silver strike, they packed up their picks and pans. They could never shake the faith that, this time, they would be the ones to get lucky. Through the rest of the nineteenth century, mineral finds drew miners to remote areas all over the West. Nevada, Colorado, Montana, Idaho, Arizona, and Alaska all had their own gold rushes.

The California Gold Rush changed the lives of nearly all those who lived through it. Among those most affected included John Sutter, on whose lands the frenzy had all begun. Sutter failed to persuade California to give him legal ownership of the land where the first gold was found. As miners flooded in and carried away the gold, Sutter lost any hope of claiming the riches as his own. The forty-niners trampled his fields and orchards, stole his cattle and horses, and ripped apart his fences for firewood. In the rush of gold-seekers, everything he owned was swept away. Soon Sutter was left with nothing. In 1880 he died in poverty, his dreams of success, like those of so many others, destroyed by gold.

Connecting East and West

"Your long looked-for letter [was] like a drop of water to a thirsty soul," wrote Lydia Burns to her sister from a California mining camp in 1853. "[W]hen all hope is gone," she continued, "[your letters give] new life to the drooping spirits and cheer me here in a strange land."

Far from their loved ones, forty-niners like Burns were often desperate for any word from home. In the early years of the gold rush, most mail was delivered by ships that traveled the long route from New York to San Francisco. Months could pass before a letter arrived, if it was not lost along the way.

Desperate for faster, more reliable mail service, 75,000 Californians signed a petition to the U.S. Congress in 1856. The government responded by offering a contract to the Overland Mail Company. The company spent a year establishing a new system for moving mail between the East and the West. It bought 250 stagecoaches, hired 800 drivers, and built 140 stations. The route the company developed began in St. Louis and ended in San Francisco. Forming a giant U-shaped loop through the Southwest, the 2,800-mile path was nicknamed the Ox Bow Route.

Beginning in 1858, stagecoaches took not only mail but also passengers west on the Ox Bow Route. Each coach had three seats inside, with enough room for nine travelers. Even with dust from the dirt road blowing in their face,

The Gadsden Purchase

In 1853 the United States acquired its last portion of western territory with the Gadsden Purchase, a small tract in what is now southern Arizona and New Mexico. The government hoped to build a railroad through the Southwest and needed to control this territory to do so. Sensing the United States' eagerness for the Gadsden Purchase, Mexico asked $10 million. The cost per acre came to a whopping $345—27 times more than the per-acre price the United States had paid for Mexican land by the Treaty of Guadalupe Hidalgo just five years before.

This engraving depicts a crowded stagecoach en route to California with passengers riding inside, in front, and on top.

some passengers preferred riding in front next to the driver to sitting in the stuffy, overcrowded cab.

Stagecoach travel was expensive. Each passenger paid two hundred dollars for the trip. The Overland Mail Company tried to make the coaches seem elegant by painting designs in gold in the interior and small landscapes on each door. But these decorative touches hardly made the 25-day trip more comfortable. To stay on schedule, the coaches traveled all day and all night, and as they bounced along rough, bumpy roads, passengers found sleeping nearly impossible. Travelers also complained of swearing, hard-drinking drivers and awful meals of beans, bacon, and bread served at the stations.

Although the Overland Mail Company was reliable, Americans clamored for even faster mail service. With another contract from the government, the Pony Express was born in April 1860. The mail system employed 120 men to ride horses loaded with mailbags from Missouri to California. To avoid overburdening the horses, riders had to be physically small, weighing no more than 135 pounds. Most of those hired were about twenty years old, but the youngest, Charlie Miller, was only eleven.

Taking a much more direct path than the Ox Bow Route, the Pony Express riders could deliver a letter in an amazing ten days. Hired for their stamina, riders covered about 75 miles before tossing their bags to the next rider waiting at a station. Every

A novel celebrating the exploits of Pony Express rider Buffalo Bill

A Pony Express rider

Western Voices

"The mail must go. Hurled by flesh and blood across 2,000 miles of desolate space—Fort Kearney, Laramie, South Pass, Fort Bridger, Salt Lake City. Neither storms, fatigue, darkness, mountains or Indians, burning sands or snow must stop the precious bags. The mail must go."

—M. Jeff Thompson, mayor of St. Joseph, Missouri, on the mission of the Pony Express in 1860

10 to 15 miles, riders stopped and changed to a fresh horse. The most skilled could dismount and jump onto their new pony in only 15 seconds.

Once in the saddle, Pony Express riders had to keep going no matter what obstacles they faced. They raced through deep rivers, over rough canyons, and across winding mountain passes. Even when blinded by snowstorms or dust clouds, they were expected to maintain their schedule. In Indian country, riders often had to move fast just to stay alive. To keep their load light, they could not carry guns, so their speed was their only protection from Indian attacks.

The Pony Express charged high fees—ten dollars for each ounce a letter weighed. Still, at first the company had little trouble finding customers willing to pay nearly any amount for ten-day service. Despite its success, however, the Pony Express lasted only 18 months. As its riders raced across the country, they watched men stringing lines for the telegraph—the invention that would soon put them out of a job.

THE TREATY OF FORT LARAMIE

In the fall of 1851, some ten thousand Plains Indians gathered in a grassy valley outside Fort Laramie, a U.S. army post in present-day Wyoming. They had been called to a "big talk" by Thomas Fitzpatrick, an agent employed by the federal government to oversee the Indians of the northern Plains. To the Indians, Fitzpatrick was known as Broken Hand, because he had lost three fingers when a gun he was holding misfired.

The goal of the Fort Laramie meeting was to keep peace on the Plains. Because of the California Gold Rush, the trickle of traffic along the overland trails had grown into a flood. Whites on the trails angered Indians by driving wagons through their territory, cutting down trees, and killing the buffalo the Indians relied on for their food. Even worse, the whites brought new diseases onto the Plains. Deadly cholera had already whipped through Indian country.

Fitzpatrick negotiated the Treaty of Fort Laramie of 1851 with the Lakota Sioux, Cheyenne, Arapaho, Crow, Arikara, Assiniboin, Mandan, and Hidatsa. He showed them a

The Indian camp near Fort Laramie, painted by American artist Alfred Jacob Miller

crude map, sketching out the U.S. government's understanding of each tribe's lands. He asked the Indians to promise never to leave their territory or fight with whites or with one another.

Under pressure from Fitzpatrick, a few Indians signed the treaty, but its rules made little sense to any of them. They lived by hunting buffalo and had to follow the great herds wherever they traveled. As long as the buffalo could not be confined within borders drawn on a map, neither would the Indians.

The Indians of the Plains were great warriors, fiercely proud of

their skill in battle. The treaty would do nothing to stop them from battling their enemies—Indian or non-Indian. At the conference, Lakota Sioux leader Black Hawk made the point that, in this way, they had much in common with Americans. Angry because Fitzpatrick's map marked as Crow territory lands the Lakota considered their own, he insisted "those lands once belonged to the Crows, but we whipped those nations out of them. And in this we did what the white men do when they want the lands of the Indians."

The telegraph was invented in 1844 by Samuel F. B. Morse. By profession he was an artist, not a scientist, but his fascination with electricity led him to devote 12 years to experimenting with it. Morse knew that electrical impulses could travel long distances along a wire. He created both an instrument to send these impulses and a code that translated them into messages. In Morse Code, each letter of the alphabet was represented by a unique pattern of long impulses (called dashes) and short impulses (called dots). In 1844 Morse finally sent the first message by telegraph between two cities.

For years the government left it to private companies to wire the nation. Slowly, cities were connected to other cities, but no company had the resources to build a telegraph that would link the East and West. Finally, in 1860 Congress

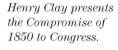

Henry Clay presents the Compromise of 1850 to Congress.

Western Voices

"There is a power in this nation greater than either the North or the South—a growing, increasing, swelling power, that will be able to speak the law to the nation. . . . That power is the country known as the great West."

—Senator Daniel Webster, arguing in favor of the Compromise of 1850

offered $40,000 a year for the next ten years to any firm that would construct a telegraph between Missouri and California. The Overland Telegraph Company began working west to east while the Pacific Telegraph Company began working east to west. In Salt

Lake City on October 24, 1861, the companies' lines were joined, and the first telegraph stretching across the West was completed. Only five years had passed since the Overland stagecoaches began their mail runs. In that short period, the time a message took to travel from coast to coast had gone from weeks to days to seconds.

Bleeding Kansas

While the stagecoach and telegraph were bringing the East and West closer together, something else was pulling the country apart—the issue of slavery. In the Southeast slavery was legal. In the Northeast it was not. When the United States acquired lands in the West after the Mexican-American War (1846–1848), Americans were faced

with a difficult question. Should this new territory be open to slavery or not?

The issue was laid to rest, at least for a time, by the Compromise of 1850. Through this law, Congress decided that California would become a free state, where slavery would be illegal. The rest of the land obtained from Mexico would become two territories—New Mexico and Utah. As their populations grew, they too could apply for statehood. According to the compromise, their citizens would decide for themselves whether they would allow slavery in their states.

The Compromise of 1850 settled some questions, but not all. A large tract of western land that the United States had obtained through the Louisiana Purchase was still not part of any state or territory. In 1854 Senator Stephen Douglas of Illinois proposed organizing the tract into the territories of Kansas

Missouri settlers crossing the state border to cast illegal pro-slavery votes in a Kansas election

John Brown

and Nebraska. He had invested money in a business to build a railroad through this land. To make that happen, territorial governments had to be in place to manage the project.

According to an older law, the Missouri Compromise of 1820, slavery was supposed to be illegal in Kansas Territory. But to win southern approval of his plan, Douglas said that the people of Kansas and Nebraska, like those in New Mexico and Utah, should be able to make their own decision about slavery. Even though many northerners spoke out against it, Douglas's proposal was passed into law as the Kansas-Nebraska Act in 1854.

Kansas suddenly became a place where the fight for or against slavery would be waged. Everything hinged on the election of the officials who would run the territory. If they were proslavery, slaves would be permitted. If officials were antislavery, slaves would be forbidden.

Most of the settlers in Kansas wanted it to be a free territory. They did not oppose slavery because they thought it was wrong. But they wanted to keep slaves out of Kansas because they did not want rich slave owners controlling the area's farmland. The Kansas settlers were mostly small farmers who could not afford to compete with plantations operated by free slave labor.

These settlers were soon joined by abolitionists from the North, who were against slavery on principle. About 1,200 abolitionists went to Kansas with the help of the New England Emigrant Aid Company. This organization was formed to transport antislavery settlers to Kansas just so they could vote to keep it a free territory. One New England emigrant, Julia Louisa Lovejoy, passionately wrote

of her mission: "Kansas is the great battlefield where a mighty conflict is to be waged with the monster slavery, and he will be routed and slain."

The efforts of the New England Emigrant Aid Company alarmed southerners, who decided to bring their own supporters into Kansas to make sure the election went their way. On election day, five thousand men from Missouri, a slave state, crossed the border into Kansas to fill the ballot box with votes for proslavery candidates. Because of these illegal voters, Kansas became a slave territory. Its new government passed a law that made even criticizing slavery illegal.

The Kansas settlers were furious. They refused to acknowledge the government voted in by Missourians, and in protest they held their own election to choose their own antislavery leaders. Kansas now had two governments, each enraged with the other.

Their mutual hatred soon erupted into violence. In the town of Lawrence, a proslavery sheriff was shot in the

Western Voices

"All here is excitement and confusion. We have just heard of the murder on Saturday night of Allen Wilkinson, Doyle and his two brothers. . . . Wilkinson, it is said, was taken from his bed, leaving a sick wife and children, and butchered in their sight. The two young Doyles were unarmed, and shot down on the prairie like dogs."

—settler William A. Heiskell, in an 1856 letter to the governor of Kansas Territory

back. The proslavery government then sent eight hundred men to arrest the antislavery leaders. They paraded through the town, destroying its two newspaper offices and looting and burning homes. The bloodshed in Lawrence soon spilled over to Washington, D.C. After Massachusetts senator Charles Sumner spoke out against the events in Kansas, Preston Brooks, a southern congressman, beat him 30 times on the head with a gold-tipped cane on the senate floor.

In Kansas, the events in Lawrence also infuriated a man named John Brown, who believed God had called him to fight slavery with violence. Telling his followers, "We must fight fire with fire," he led a group that included his four sons to a settlement on Pottawatomie Creek. Brown's band seized five men they thought were part of the proslavery faction and hacked

them to death with swords. None of the victims, however, had had anything to do with the raid on Lawrence.

The war in Kansas continued for months, with neighbor shooting at neighbor. Before U.S. troops could end the fighting, two hundred people had died and more than two million dollars' worth of property had been destroyed. The violence earned the territory the nickname Bleeding Kansas.

Many Americans had hoped that the opening of the West would somehow resolve the conflicts between the North and the South. But as the events in Kansas showed, the troubles were only growing worse. Soon it would be clear that the killing in Kansas was just the beginning. In a matter of years, as Americans took up arms against one another, not only Kansas, but the entire country, would be bleeding.

Men from the antislavery faction in Kansas preparing for a fight in 1856

CHAPTER FIVE

THE STRUGGLE FOR CONTROL

1861 to 1876

I n 1861 the debate over slavery erupted into a full-scale war—the Civil War. On one side was the Confederacy, proslavery southern states that wished to break away, or secede, from the rest of America and form their own nation. On the other was the Union, antislavery northern states that wanted the United States to remain united. Most westerners supported the Union.

The Civil War in the West

T he only western state to join the Confederacy was Texas, which had been settled mostly by southern farmers who used slaves to work their fields. Not surprisingly, they sympathized with the South and the proslavery cause.

Just weeks after the war began, a Confederate army of 3,500 Texans took over the U.S. army forts in their state. They then headed southwest into New Mexico Territory (now the states of New Mexico and Arizona). For years Texas had eyed New Mexico and its dry but rich farmland. Now, the war gave Texans an excuse to invade the territory and make it their own. Taking over the towns of Albuquerque and Santa Fe, they renamed the territory the Confederate State of Arizona.

Led by Henry H. Sibley, the Texans then set their sights on an even greater

◀ *Opposite page: Workers building the transcontinental railroad, photographed in 1869*

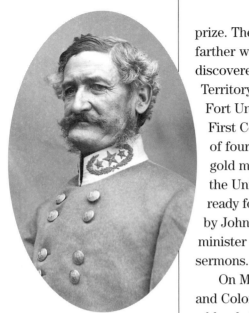

Henry H. Sibley

prize. They were determined to move farther west and take control of recently discovered goldfields in Colorado Territory. Standing in their way was Fort Union—a post occupied by the First Colorado Volunteers, a regiment of four thousand Coloradans, mostly gold miners, who had recently joined the Union army. Barely trained but ready for a fight, they were commanded by John M. Chivington, a Methodist minister well known for his fiery sermons.

On March 26–28, 1862, the Texans and Coloradans met at Glorieta Pass in a bloody battle that lasted five hours before the Texans admitted defeat. During the fight, Chivington's troops managed to destroy 85 wagons full of the enemy's food and supplies. As the defeated Confederate army retreated to Texas, the men had almost nothing to

eat or drink. Hiking over the burning sands of the southwestern desert, almost half of the Texans died. With that horrible loss, the Confederacy's dream of conquering the Southwest died.

In the meantime, the Civil War was being fought on another western front along the border of Kansas and Missouri. Although Missouri was a slave state, it did not formally join the Confederacy. Confederate leaders hoped to invade the state with the help of the large tribes living in nearby Indian Territory, including several from the Southeast. Even though southerners had forced the Indians out of their own homelands in the 1830s, they still had ties to the South. And like most wealthy southerners, many prominent men in Indian Territory were slave owners. They had much to lose personally if the Confederacy lost the war.

Quantrill's Raiders burning the town of Lawrence, Kansas, in 1863

Some Indian groups, such as the Choctaw and Chickasaw, were eager to pledge allegiance to the South. Others, such as the Creek and Seminole, joined the Confederacy even though many tribe members disagreed with the decision. The Cherokee, though, tried to stay out of the war altogether. Their principal chief, John Ross, thought nothing good could come from Cherokee involvement. Yet, even Ross gave up his neutral stance when the Union pulled its troops out of Indian Territory. With no military protection, Ross feared Confederate soldiers would invade the Cherokee Nation unless the tribe sided with the South. To Ross, the Cherokee seemed like "a man standing upon a low naked spot of ground with the water rising all around him" as a log floats by. "By refusing [the log] he is a doomed man," Ross wrote. "By seizing hold of it he has a chance for his life."

Indian troops joined Confederate soldiers in the Battle of Pea Ridge, fought March 6–8, 1862, in northwest Arkansas. The Confederate forces hoped to invade southern Missouri, but had to retreat when they ran out of ammunition. Officially, the Union still held Missouri, but long-festering tensions between the people of Missouri and Kansas soon exploded into violence. Antislavery Kansans called Jayhawkers began looting and burning Missouri settlements. Proslavery Missourians called Bushwhackers fought back with attacks on Kansas towns.

The worst fighting occurred on August 21, 1863, when a band of 450 young men—mostly teenagers—rode into Lawrence, Kansas, where many antislavery leaders lived. The gang was led by William C. Quantrill, a captain in the Confederate army who had a taste for violence. He commanded his followers to "kill every male and burn every house" in town. While he ate breakfast at the town's hotel, Quantrill's Raiders did their bloody work, murdering more than 150 men and trapping others in their burning homesteads. Many were slaughtered as their wives and children watched. The Union army retaliated by driving Missouri Confederates from their settlements, leaving Jayhawkers to set ablaze the houses and fields they left behind. The area was so ravaged by fire that for years it was called the Burnt District.

Invaded by Union troops in the summer of 1863, Indian Territory suffered a similar fate. Indian nations there were left in ruins as gangs of Union and Confederate deserters roamed the countryside, killing and looting. The worst losses were experienced by the Cherokee, Creek,

The Immovable Stand Watie

During the Civil War era, one of the most important people in the Cherokee Nation was Stand Watie. His name came from the Cherokee word *takertawker*, meaning "immovable." Certainly, Watie's opinions could not be easily swayed. He openly defied Chief John Ross by speaking out against Ross's efforts to remain neutral in the Civil War. Largely due to Watie's influence, the Cherokee were persuaded to side with the Confederacy.

Watie himself took to the battlefield. As a brigadier general, he earned the highest rank of any Indian in the Confederate army. A fighter to the end, Watie became the last of all the Confederate generals to surrender, on June 23, 1865.

A Lakota Sioux delegation led by Red Cloud (center) that traveled to Washington, D.C., to meet with President Ulysses S. Grant. The Indians' interpreter stands behind them.

and Seminole. One out of every four of their tribe members died during the war.

The war's end in April 1865 brought little relief. As Chief John Ross had feared, the Cherokee and the other Confederate-allied tribes had chosen the wrong side. The victorious Union now insisted they sign punishing peace treaties. With their nations nearly destroyed, Ross and other tribal leaders were forced to hand over half of their lands in Indian Territory to the U.S. government.

Fighting Indians

With the exception of the Indian Territory tribes, most western Indians had nothing to do with the Civil War. Many, however, were drawn into bloody conflicts with American troops during the war years. Particularly eager to fight Indians were the army's freshest recruits. Because all experienced soldiers were sent east to fight in the war, young, untrained volunteers took their place at western forts, often with violent results.

A war with the Lakota Sioux broke out in the early 1860s along the Bozeman Trail, a route that took travelers from Julesburg, an old mining town in Colorado Territory, just west of the Bighorn Mountains, to goldfields in present-day Montana. The path cut straight through the Lakota's traditional hunting territory, and the Lakota were annoyed by the whites' invasion of their lands. But they were furious when U.S. army troops built three forts—Fort Reno, Fort Phil Kearney, and Fort C. F. Smith—along the trail. Led by Red Cloud, Lakota warriors continually harassed the soldiers. After years of talks with U.S.

negotiators, Red Cloud forced the United States to agree to his own terms for peace. In the Treaty of Fort Laramie of 1868, the government promised to abandon the Bozeman Trail forts if Red Cloud called off his fighters.

To the north in Minnesota, the Dakota (often called the Santee Sioux) rebelled against the United States with far worse results. Pushed from their lands by white settlers, the Dakota were confined to small reservations, designated areas that they were given to live in. The U.S. government promised to provide them rations of food, but in the summer of 1862, the Dakota were close to starvation. They pleaded with the government's agent on the reservation, but he refused to give them anything. A friend of the agent quoted him as saying, "So far as I am concerned, if they are hungry let them eat grass!" The desperate Dakota, led by Little Crow, responded by attacking nearby settlers, killing more than four hundred whites before they were subdued. On December 26, 38 of the Dakota rebels were hanged in the largest public execution in American history.

In the Southwest, the Mescalero Apache and the Navajo were also caught up in a war with army troops. In 1862

CYNTHIA PARKER

On December 18, 1860, U.S. soldiers stormed into a Comanche Indian camp on the Pease River in Texas. The Indians there had been looting American settlements nearby, and the troops were determined to make them pay. Even though most of the group's men were away hunting, the soldiers shot anyone they could, mostly unarmed women and children. One soldier took aim at a young Comanche mother carrying a baby girl. Seeing the soldier, the mother shouted "Americanos," in the desperate hope that the man would not murder a fellow American.

The woman was Cynthia Ann Parker. In 1836, when she was nine, the Comanche had attacked her family's homestead, killing five people, including her father. Cynthia was taken captive and, following Indian custom, adopted into the tribe. Over the years, the surviving Parkers tried several times to pay a ransom for Cynthia's return. The Comanche refused, saying Cynthia wanted to stay with them.

During the Pease River attack, the soldiers spared the life of Cynthia and her daughter Topsannah and took them to live with Cynthia's uncle. Newspapers declared that at last Cynthia Parker had been rescued. Cynthia, however, was terrified of white people and miserable in their company and just wanted to go home to her Comanche husband and relatives. Her grief grew even deeper when Topsannah died in 1863. Cynthia Parker lived for seven more years before she finally starved herself to death. Her son Quanah grew up to become one of the Comanche's greatest leaders.

Quanah Parker

This group of Navajo were among the eight thousand sent to live on the Bosque Redondo reservation.

Brigadier General James H. Carleton of the California Volunteers was placed in charge of the army in New Mexico Territory. Determined to make a name for himself, Carleton began battling Indians there. The war against the Navajo was particularly brutal. On Carleton's orders, Union Colonel Christopher "Kit" Carson destroyed fields, orchards, and hogans and then forced the Navajo to seek refuge in Canyon de Chelly, where they were trapped. In 1864, after their surrender, eight thousand Navajo were forced to march hundreds of miles across the desert and placed on a barren reservation called Bosque Redondo. The march, known to the Navajo as the Long Walk, was one of the bleakest moments in the tribe's history.

Like Carleton, Colonel John M. Chivington sought fame by provoking war with western Indians. In the summer of 1861, he had become a war hero by leading Union forces against the Confederate Texans at the Battle of Glorieta Pass. His image began to

suffer, though, when he assumed command of the Third Colorado Cavalry, whose undisciplined volunteers were supposed to protect Coloradans from Indian attack. When after three months no one had fired a shot, the

Western Voices

"There was one little child, probably three years old, just big enough to walk through the sand. The Indians had gone ahead, and this little child was behind following them. The little fellow was perfectly naked, traveling on the sand. I saw one man get off his horse . . . and draw up his rifle and fire—he missed the child. Another man came up . . . but he missed him. A third man came up . . . and fired, and the little fellow dropped."

—*U.S. Army Major Scott Anthony, on the 1864 Sand Creek Massacre*

cavalry became a laughingstock. Newspapers mocked Chivington's unit as the "Bloodless Third."

Eager for a fight, Chivington and his seven hundred men staged a dawn attack on a group of Southern Cheyenne camped

Black Kettle (seated, far left) with a delegation of Southern Cheyenne and Arapaho leaders

along Sand Creek. The Indians' leader, Black Kettle, had met the Colorado Territory's governor for peace talks with the Americans just two months before. As Chivington's soldiers rode into the camp, both an American flag and a white flag of surrender were flying on a post outside Black Kettle's tepee.

Chivington's soldiers, though, cared little whether these Southern Cheyenne were friends or enemies; the commander just wanted to show that his men were not afraid to fight, that they were not bloodless. The soldiers murdered every Indian they could find—men, women, and children—and left behind more than two hundred corpses, many scalped and cut to pieces.

As news of the Sand Creek Massacre spread, many easterners protested the senseless slaughter. But in Colorado Territory, where hatred of

In 1866 the U.S. Congress established six regiments of African-American soldiers to help police the West. Mostly former slaves, these troops were dubbed buffalo soldiers by the Cheyenne and were stationed in the most isolated and dangerous posts in the West. Generally paid less than white soldiers for the same work, the buffalo soldiers were also given the worst equipment and horses, usually castoffs from white regiments. Despite the difficulties they faced, many buffalo soldiers distinguished themselves for their courage and skill. Eighteen were awarded the Congressional Medal of Honor for their bravery.

Perhaps the most distinguished buffalo soldier was Charles Young. A graduate of West Point Military Academy, Young had a successful 30-year career that included service as a commander during the Spanish-American War (1898). After his death in 1922, he was buried at Arlington National Cemetery with full military honors.

The Sand Creek Massacre, *painted by Robert Lindneux*

Speculating in Homesteads

One of the goals of the Homestead Act of 1862 was to put land speculators out of business. These speculators bought up western farmland cheaply and later resold it to farm families for a big profit. Homesteaders resented speculators, who often made huge amounts of money for doing almost nothing while the homesteaders worked hard to develop their land.

To deter speculators, the Homestead Act required that people claiming land settle on it themselves. Clever speculators, though, found a way of avoiding this rule by hiring phony homesteaders to make claims on their behalf. These employees built rickety cabins and stayed on their claims for six months. At that time they qualified to buy the land at a bargain rate. Using money from the speculators who had hired them, the phony homesteaders bought their cheap plots, then turned over the deeds to the land to the employers, receiving a small fee in return. Through these shady dealings, speculators took advantage of the Homestead Act.

Indians ran deep, whites celebrated Chivington and his troops. They were cheered in a parade through the streets of Denver while scalps of their Indian victims hung in the city's opera house for all to see.

Homesteading

In the early nineteenth century, few Americans thought to settle in the Great Plains, the dry, grassy area that includes portions of present-day Montana, North Dakota, South Dakota, Kansas, Nebraska, Oklahoma, Texas, Iowa, and Missouri. Most people thought the region was too difficult to live in because the land was not well suited for farming. In most schoolbooks of the day, the area was labeled not the Great Plains, but the Great American Desert.

Western Voices

"The jam was terrible. . . . The applications poured in as fast as they could be taken care of all day, the crowd inside and out never growing smaller, for as fast as one applicant, with papers properly fixed up, would worm his way through the crowd to the door, and be cast out, panting and dripping with perspiration, another would squeeze in."

—*Nebraska settler Beatrice Express, on applying for a homestead in 1871*

After the Civil War, though, farmers began giving the area another look. The Plains did not offer the best farmland, but the price to buy land could not be beat. In 1862 the U.S. Congress passed

A wagon train crossing the Plains on its way to Montana

the Homestead Act, which allowed the head of a family to claim 160 acres on unsettled Plains land. If the family farmed and lived on their plot for six months, they could buy the land for a bargain price. But if the family stayed for five years, all they had to pay for the plot was a ten-dollar fee.

Many people thought the Homestead Act was a great gift to the poor, offering anyone in the East who could not find work the ability to move west and build their own farm. One of the law's greatest supporters was newspaper editor Horace Greeley, who predicted that the act would turn all "paupers and idlers" into "working, independent, self-subsisting farmers." Advertisements trying to bring settlers to Nebraska promised "Land for the Landless! Homes for the Homeless!"

In fact, establishing a farm on the Plains took a fair amount of money. The land was almost free, but the cost of moving and of buying livestock and farm equipment mounted up quickly. Few poor eastern laborers had the savings to claim their own homestead. Instead, many homesteaders were western farming families who just wanted more land. Others came from Europe, where almost all the land was owned by the wealthy; the offer of free land in America was irresistible. European homesteaders came from many different countries, including Switzerland, Ireland, the Netherlands, France, and England. More than 60,000 Germans settled in Kansas alone.

Once a homesteading family claimed its 160 acres, its members started the hard work of making a farm. Together

A homesteading family poses proudly outside their sod house in Nebraska in about 1880.

A poster advertising available homesteads

WESTERN WOMEN AND THE VOTE

Before 1920 American women were not allowed to vote in national elections. But many western states gave women the vote far earlier. The first was Wyoming in 1869, though at that time there were only about one thousand adult women in the state—too few to make much of a difference. One journalist noted that giving women the vote in Wyoming had about as much effect as giving it to "angels or Martians." Echoing this attitude, some of the Wyoming legislators who supported the measure thought it something of a joke. Most, though, were probably trying to make the state more attractive to women. With only one woman for every six men, Wyoming men, particularly bachelors, were eager to see more women settle there.

The next year women in Utah got the vote, but for a very different reason. At the time Mormons, who made up most of Utah's population, were under attack for practicing polygamy—allowing a man to have more than one wife. Many outsiders thought polygamy was sinful. Some, especially eastern female reformers, said that if women were allowed to vote in Utah, they would surely outlaw the evil practice. To silence their criticism, Mormon leaders decided to push for the vote for women. As these leaders expected, Mormon women did not try to outlaw polygamy. They instead voted much as their husbands did.

After Wyoming and Utah gave women the vote, western women in other states started campaigning for it as well. Why western male legislators were more willing than easterners to give the vote to women is not completely clear. Perhaps because there were proportionately fewer women in the West, western men held them in greater regard. Another possibility is that the importance of women was more obvious to westerners. Much of the work of establishing a western settlement—from building houses to raising children to helping neighbors—was done by women. Granting women the vote, then, may have been merely a convenient way for western men to show their gratitude to their mothers, wives, and daughters.

Wyoming's measure set an example for other states to follow. By 1914 ten more states—all in the West—allowed women to participate in at least some local elections.

A western woman receiving the deed to her own homestead

The Grange

Families working hard to build farms on isolated homesteads often felt desperate and alone. To help them cope, Department of Agriculture clerk Oliver H. Kelley founded the Grange in 1867. Through this organization, farmers pooled their knowledge about working the land and raising livestock. Perhaps even more important, the Grange sponsored social get-togethers, where families could meet and share their hopes and fears. Through the Grange, homesteaders were given a voice in politics and the courts, eventually enabling them to push for laws that limited how much railroads could charge small farms to ship goods.

they had to clear fields, plant crops, and construct houses. Because few trees grew on the Plains, homesteaders had little wood for building. Instead they cut bricks of soil, or sod, which they then stacked to make sod houses, known as soddies. Soddies were fairly warm in winter and cool in summer, but they were always dirty because bits of soil fell from the ceiling. In a heavy downpour, their roofs often caved in.

Too much rain, though, was rarely a problem on the Plains. More often there was not enough to water the homesteaders' fields. Crops were also threatened by insects. In 1874 many homesteaders were forced to give up when their farms were overtaken by swarms of grasshoppers, so thick they looked like storm clouds. The grasshoppers destroyed any plant that sprouted. One settler remembered that they "devoured every green thing but the prairie grass."

Another problem for homesteaders was debt. Because many families came west without enough money to buy everything they needed once they got settled, they had to borrow money to buy equipment and supplies. As their debt grew, they had to work harder and harder to pay it off. Even well-financed homesteaders found they had to borrow to buy more land. With the exception of the most fertile, well-watered areas, 160 acres on the Plains could rarely produce enough food for a single family.

These Exodusters were among the African-American settlers who came to Kansas to establish their own farms.

Hard as it was, the life of a homesteader represented the best opportunity some had to make a living. In the 1870s some 20,000 African Americans left the South and went to Kansas to start their own farms. Former slaves who were still treated badly by white southerners, these African Americans saw Kansas as a promised land. They became known as the Exodusters because they compared their move to Kansas to the flight to freedom of Moses's people described in Exodus, the second book of the Bible.

Homesteading also allowed many women to live more independent lives. Between 5 and 15 percent of all homestead claims were made by unmarried women. (Married women could not claim land because by law their husbands were considered the head of their families.) One successful female homesteader, Elinore Pruitt Stewart, wrote that "any woman who can stand her own company, can see the beauty of the sunset, loves growing things, and is willing to put in as much time and careful labor as she does over the washtub, will have independence, plenty to eat all the time, and a home of her own in the end."

In reality, hard work and determination did not always guarantee that a homesteader would be successful. Only one out of three homesteader families stuck it out the full five years required to get the deed to their land. Some gave up and headed home. Others stayed in the West and labored for wages. Some men who came west with dreams of owning their own small farms instead found themselves working as hired hands on huge farms. These operations were called bonanza farms because they were so profitable. They were owned by big companies that bought up enormous amounts of Plains land. One operation in North Dakota covered more land than two hundred homesteader farms.

GOING TO TOWN

In the late nineteenth century, many western towns were little more than a dusty unpaved main street, lined with a general store, blacksmith shop, hotel, and saloon or two. However small, a town could still be an exciting place for homesteaders to visit. Used to being alone on their isolated farms, in town they could enjoy a little conversation and gossip with their neighbors while they shopped for needed supplies.

As towns grew, they offered more and more attractions. Main Street might feature a drugstore, clothing shops, and restaurants. The general store might expand to offer customers a wider variety of goods. One proprietor boasted that his store stocked everything from "a $500 diamond ring to a pint of salt."

Towns also offered an array of entertainment. Sports lovers could watch a boxing match or play a baseball game, and the civic-minded could attend political rallies and speeches during election years. Everyone could enjoy shows put on by traveling performers—from Shakespearean actors to magicians to brass bands. Speaking for many people living in western towns and the surrounding countryside, a journalist in Omaha in Nebraska Territory wrote in 1866 that "we are always gratified to see a responsible and legitimate amusement come here and carry off our surplus dollars and dimes."

This store in a Nebraska town provided nearby farm families with the goods they needed, from paint to bullets to schoolbooks.

Chinese workers, like these constructing a trestle through the Sierras in 1877, helped build the first transcontinental railroad.

Building the Railroad

In 1862, the same year Congress passed the Homestead Act, it stamped approval on another equally important law—the Pacific Railroad Act. In it, the U.S. government promised to help fund a railroad across the West. The homesteaders and the railroad needed each other: Without a railroad, homesteaders could not get their crops to market once their farms were up and running. And without the homesteaders, railroads would not have enough customers to turn a profit.

By the 1860s there were many small railroad companies operating in the East. The goal of the Pacific Railroad Act was to connect these to a line running from Omaha, Nebraska, to Sacramento, California. With this line in place, a passenger could travel by rail all the way from the east coast to the west coast. The United States would then have its first transcontinental railroad—

a system that stretched all the way across the North American continent.

The government contracted two railroad companies to do the work. The Union Pacific would lay track westward from Omaha. The Central Pacific would work eastward from Sacramento. Somewhere in the middle—no one knew exactly where—the two lines would meet, and the transcontinental railroad would be complete.

The work started slowly. In its first two years, the Union Pacific managed to lay only 40 miles of track; but after the Civil War ended in 1865, the companies quickened the pace because soldiers without jobs were eager to take work with the railroads. Even so, the railroad companies had to look abroad to find enough laborers. In addition to former

African-American slaves, most of the Union Pacific's workers were poor Irishmen and Mexicans. Because there were few laborers for hire in California, the Central Pacific recruited most of its employees from China.

More difficult than hiring enough laborers was finding enough money to build the railroad. Buying the necessary iron and wood and carting it west on boats and wagons was hugely expensive. The federal government responded by footing much of the bill. It gave the companies the land they needed outright. It also lent them money for each mile of track laid. The government paid $16,000 per mile through flatland and $48,000 per mile through the mountains. These measures started a frenzied race between the Central Pacific and the Union

Much of the money spent on the railroads went right into the pockets of their owners. Some stockholders of the Union Pacific railroad, for instance, became wildly rich by establishing Crédit Mobilier. This company received money from Union Pacific contracts, which overcharged for the work done. While the railroad showed no profits at all, Crédit Mobilier made a fortune of $7 million to $23 million for its owners. To keep the arrangement quiet, the company bribed Vice President Schuyler Colfax and several of the most important members of Congress. In 1872, shortly before the presidential election, a reporter broke the story, which became one of the biggest scandals in U.S. history.

Vice President Schuyler Colfax (seated center) with family and friends in Utah in 1869. During the Crédit Mobilier Scandal, it was revealed that Colfax took bribes from the Union Pacific Railroad.

PICTURING THE WEST

The highest mountains, the widest valleys, the whitest clouds—all were depicted in the huge western paintings of Albert Bierstadt. Born in Germany in 1830, Bierstadt, when still a baby, moved with his family to New Bedford, Massachusetts. As a young man he traveled to Europe to study art and was inspired by the beauty of the Alps mountain range in Switzerland. When he returned to the United States, Bierstadt was determined to see the "American Alps"—the Rocky Mountains. In 1859 he joined a surveying expedition and spent the summer sketching the Rockies.

On his return east, Bierstadt opened a studio in New York City. Working on enormous canvases as wide as 15 feet, he painted a series of landscapes based on his sketches, memory, and imagination. Bierstadt did not paint exactly what he had seen. Instead, he created dramatic scenes based on actual places.

Bierstadt's paintings of the Rockies were enormously successful; collectors were willing to pay for one painting as much as $25,000—about half a million dollars in today's money. Bierstadt's timing was just right: In the 1860s many Americans in the East were

desperate to see the scenery of the West that most had only read about. Still, some people found Bierstadt's works too overblown and unreal.

After the transcontinental railroad was built in 1869, however, his paintings quickly went out of favor. Traveling by rail, more Americans began to see the West with their own eyes and to their surprise, the real West barely resembled Bierstadt's. His work became so unfashionable that he was all but forgotten when he died in 1902. Only recently has the public taken a second look. Many of his works are today considered masterpieces.

In the Yosemite Valley
by Albert Bierstadt, 1866

Pacific: Whichever company laid the most track would make the most money.

At first the Central Pacific had the harder job. Working west to east from California, its Chinese laborers had to make their way through the Sierra Nevada. Many were given only pickaxes to chip away the mountains, one rock at a time. Others had the incredibly dangerous task of blasting through the thick rock faces with explosives.

The Chinese railroad workers were well regarded by their employers for their hard work and sobriety. Unlike many other laborers for the Union Pacific, they shunned whiskey dealers and gamblers who swarmed into the huge camps of tents set up for workers. The Union Pacific tent towns were filled with wild behavior and lawlessness, and more men died from brawls and disease in these filthy camps than from accidents on the job. After visiting the tent town of Julesburg, in present-day Colorado, one journalist wrote, "I verily believe that there are men here who would murder a fellow creature for five dollars. Nay, there are men who have already done it."

During their working hours, though, laborers with both companies were driven hard. By early 1869 the two groups were racing toward each other at breakneck speed, each company desperate to lay more track than the other. Even as they passed each other in present-day Utah, neither company was willing to give up the race. Both were more interested in collecting additional money and land from the government

A wagon train carrying supplies to railroad construction crews

Promontory Point in Utah was chosen as the spot where the two lines of the transcontinental railroad would meet.

than joining their two railroad lines. Quality also went by the wayside. The work on the first transcontinental railroad was so shoddy that some ten million dollars' worth of labor would later be needed to fix it.

Finally, President Ulysses S. Grant ended the game. He ordered the Union Pacific and the Central Pacific to make their lines meet at Promontory Point in what is now Utah. There, on May 10, 1869, hundreds gathered for the Golden Spike Ceremony. They jockeyed to get the best view of Central Pacific investor Leland Stanford, who, using a silver mallet, was to drive in the last railroad spike. Made of solid gold, the spike was attached to a telegraph wire so that as it was struck, the sound would be sent throughout the nation. A better businessman than railroad worker, Stanford missed the spike entirely, so

The crowd gathered to celebrate the driving of the Golden Spike

the word *done* had to be sent over the telegraph instead. Yet at the news, Americans everywhere cheered, rang church bells, and shot off cannons in celebration as they heard that the East and West were at last connected by rail.

YELLOWSTONE NATIONAL PARK

Tourists vacationing in Yellowstone National Park in the 1880s

In the early nineteenth century, mountain men who had roamed along the Yellowstone River in present-day Wyoming told amazing stories about the region. They described enormous canyons, roaring waterfalls, and great hot springs that shot water high into the sky. Most who heard their stories dismissed them as tall tales until a scientific expedition traveled to Yellowstone in 1871. This Geological and Geographical Survey expedition, headed by geologist Ferdinand V. Hayden, included two artists, painter Thomas Moran and photographer William Henry Jackson.

Accompanying Hayden's official report, their images of the Yellowstone region showed that what the mountain men had said was true. The area was full of natural wonders more spectacular than most Americans had ever even imagined.

The exciting news was particularly interesting to Jay Cooke, owner of the Northern Pacific Railroad, who proposed to Congress that it set aside the Yellowstone region as "a public park forever." Cooke had his own reasons for making the suggestion: He hoped that creating a Yellowstone park would increase his business. He believed eastern tourists would be eager to visit the park, especially if they could make the trip in a comfortable railroad car. On March 1, 1872, Congress accepted Cooke's proposal and designated more than two million acres of land on the Yellowstone River as a "pleasuring ground for the benefit and enjoyment of the people," thereby creating the United States' first national park.

On the Plains, the railroads disrupted the movements of the great buffalo herds that Indians relied on for food and other necessities.

Indians' Uses of Buffalo Parts

Hides: tepee covers, clothing, and storage bags

Hoofs: glue and ceremonial rattles

Fat: candles and soap

Horns: spoons and bowls

Bones: tools and arrowheads

Hair: ropes and pillow stuffing

Dung: fuel

Tongue: combs

The War for the Plains

Not everyone was thrilled by the new transcontinental railroad. For the Indian nations of the Plains, the railroad brought trouble, as more and more non-Indians invaded their lands. In addition to settlers, white hunters were soon streaming in by rail.

These hunters came to the Plains in search of the enormous buffalo herds that roamed the region. Indian groups such as the Lakota Sioux, Cheyenne, and Arapaho were also buffalo hunters. By using every part of the buffalo—from its meat to its horns to its hides—they had everything they needed to survive. White buffalo hunters, however, wanted the animals for only one thing—their skins. Buffalo fur blankets had become fashionable, so their skins could be sold at a high price. After 1870, when a new process was developed to turn buffalo hides to leather, the skins were also in demand to make leather belts for factory machines.

Often shooting from the windows of train cars, white hunters set out to kill as many buffalo as they could. One hunter named William F. Cody—later known as Buffalo Bill—bragged that he shot down 4,300 animals in just one year. When whites stripped off the skin of their prey, they usually left the body to rot in

Western Voices

"Your people make big talk, and sometimes make war, if an Indian kills a white man's ox to keep his wife and children from starving; what do you think my people ought to say when they see their [buffalo] killed by your race when you are not hungry?"

—Cheyenne leader Little Robe, on the slaughter of the buffalo in the 1870s

the sun. Soon the Plains were covered with bloody, stinking animal carcasses. This display disgusted the Indians, who considered the white hunters' wastefulness an insult to the Creator.

Many army men policing the West encouraged the slaughter. Because the Indians' way of life depended so heavily on the buffalo, these soldiers believed that as the number of buffalo fell, so would the number of Indians on the Plains. As one colonel put it, "Every buffalo dead is an Indian gone."

By the mid-1870s there were no buffalo left on the southern Plains, and many Indians living there felt they had no choice but to move onto the reservations assigned to them by the United States. There, the meager food rations handed out by government agents would at least keep them from starving. However, some Lakota leaders, such as Crazy Horse and Sitting Bull, refused to give up their old ways.

Speaking angrily to reservation Indians, Sitting Bull declared, "You are fools to make yourselves slaves to a piece of fat bacon . . . and a little sugar and coffee."

Supposedly to keep an eye on these Indian resisters, a group of soldiers led by Lieutenant Colonel George Armstrong Custer rode into Lakota Sioux country in 1874. In fact, they were looking for gold. Rumors had been spreading that a great stash of the precious metal could be found in the Black Hills, an area

White hunters shooting buffalo from a train

Buffalo heads displayed outside a Kansas Pacific railway station

A painting of the Battle of
Little Bighorn by Lakota
artist Kicking Bear

George Armstrong Custer

sacred to the Lakota and other Indian groups. A flashy dresser proud of his long blond hair, Custer was eager to make a name for himself. When his men found gold, he did not hesitate to telegraph a New York newspaper to announce that there was "gold among the roots of the grass." His words started a Black Hills gold rush.

Under the terms of the 1868 Treaty of Fort Laramie, the U.S. army was supposed to keep whites out of the region. But the soldiers mostly turned their backs, allowing thousands of miners to flood illegally into sacred Lakota territory. The U.S. government figured it could easily buy the valuable Black Hills from the Indians once the land had been overrun by whites. The Lakota, however, turned down six million dollars, saying the land was not for sale at any price.

The army struck back at the Lakota. Officers announced that any Indian who did not move to a reservation by January 31, 1876, would be hunted down. The deadline came and went. Sitting Bull, Crazy Horse, and their followers still refused to stay within the reservation borders. By June thousands of U.S. soldiers had reached the resisters'

stronghold in Montana Territory. Both sides were ready for battle.

Their first encounter was at the Rosebud River on June 17, when about 1,200 Lakota and Cheyenne warriors attacked a camp of an equal number of soldiers under the command of General George Crook. The battle lasted a full six hours before the Indians retreated. Although neither side had won a clear victory, the Battle of the Rosebud dealt a serious blow to the U.S. army. The troops involved suffered so many casualties that they could not fight for more than a month. As a result, they were unable to serve as reinforcements for Custer at the Battle of Little Bighorn, which followed shortly.

After the Rosebud encounter, Crazy Horse's force crossed to the Little Bighorn Valley, where they joined thousands of other Indians. Custer, leading the Seventh Cavalry, was sent to find the Indians' camp. On the Little Bighorn River, he spied a group of tepees. Hungry for glory, Custer did not want to miss a chance to score a brilliant victory. He ordered his men to rush the camp instead of waiting for more soldiers to arrive.

On June 25 Custer's troops rode toward the Little Bighorn and were almost immediately surrounded by thousands of Lakota and Cheyenne. In minutes, Custer and his men—about 225 in all—were dead.

For the Indians, the victory was sweet, if short-lived. News of the Battle of Little Bighorn aroused Americans across the country, many of whom demanded that the Plains be wiped clean of Indians once and for all. The army responded by pursuing the Indians living outside reservations more fiercely than ever before. They prevented them from hunting and refused to give their reservation kin the rations due to them by treaty. Desperate and hungry, the chiefs on the reservation agreed to give the Black Hills to the United States by the end of 1876. Sitting Bull and his followers escaped to Canada, and by the spring Crazy Horse agreed to live on a reservation. Although he surrendered, his spirit of resistance remained strong.

Sitting Bull

Within months, the ever-proud warrior was dead at age thirty-six, stabbed by a white man's bayonet.

A meeting between Geronimo (third from the left) and George Crook (second from the right)

George Crook and Geronimo

In 1882 a group of Chiricahua Apache led by Geronimo escaped from San Carlos Reservation in Arizona Territory. As they hid in Mexico's Sierra Madre, General George Crook was ordered to lure them out. Apache scouts took him to Geronimo's stronghold, located deep in the mountains. Exhausted by life on the run, the Chiricahua surrendered and returned to San Carlos.

But living conditions on the reservation were so difficult that Geronimo and his band fled once again in 1886. Crook was relieved of his command and replaced by Nelson A. Miles. General Miles found Geronimo and told him that if he gave up, he and his people would be allowed to return to San Carlos. As soon as Geronimo surrendered, however, Miles put the Chiricahua in chains and sent them to a prison in Florida.

Crook was outraged by Miles's dishonesty. He spent the rest of his life demanding that the U.S. government release Geronimo and his people. The Lakota leader Red Cloud voiced the respect that many Indians felt for Crook with the words, "He never lied to us. His words gave the people hope."

CHAPTER SIX

CLOSING THE OPEN RANGE

1877 to 1890

As buffalo were disappearing from the Plains, other animals—cattle— began taking their place. Cattle had first come to North America with Spanish explorers in the sixteenth century. From enslaved Africans, the Spanish learned to raise cattle in the Southwest, grazing the animals on the grasses that grew there naturally. Over time, many of the cattle escaped from their masters. By the mid-nineteenth century, they had grown into a great wild herd. There were as many as five million head of cattle roaming the countryside of north Texas alone.

The Cowboy Life

In Texas, calves (baby cattle) sold for about six dollars each. But in the northern Plains, adult cattle ready for butchering sold for ten times that amount. There, at railroad stops such as Abilene, Kansas, the animals could be sent by rail to Chicago, Illinois, for slaughter.

Clever businessmen saw an opportunity to make money as ranchers. They bought herds of cattle cheaply in Texas and hired teams of laborers to drive them north. On the way, the animals

◄ *Opposite page: Settlers rush to claim land in present-day Oklahoma on April 22, 1889.*

The Longhorn

"Eight pounds of hamburger on eight hundred pounds of bone and horn"—that is how cattlemen described the Texas longhorn. Descended from Spanish cattle, this breed had little meat, and what it had was tough and stringy. Still, the hardy longhorn was so easy to raise that it was at the heart of the nineteenth-century cattle industry. Longhorns needed only a little water and a little grass and could survive outdoors in the cold Plains winters. Angering longhorns, though, could be dangerous. As the name suggested, they had two great horns, stretching five feet from tip to tip. One of the hardest jobs a cowboy had was roping these great animals and clipping their horns' sharp tips.

Cowboys gather at a railroad stop, where their cattle are being loaded onto trains bound for the slaughterhouse.

could feast for free on grass and water on unsettled Plains land. When the herds reached Abilene or another cow town on a railroad line, the animals were sold at a hefty profit. One successful cattle drive could make a rancher a small fortune.

By the 1880s these businessmen had developed a thriving cattle industry. While they grew rich, their employees—called cowboys—did the work. Most cowboys were young men, some just teenagers, mostly from Texas and Louisiana, who were more interested in adventure than money. For a month's work, the average white cowboy earned about forty dollars, the equivalent of six hundred dollars today. About one third of the cowboys were African Americans, Mexicans, and Indians, and they earned even less.

For their meager wages, cowboys had to labor long and hard. In the spring and fall, their work centered on the roundup. In the early years of the cattle industry, there were no pens or fences to keep one cattleman's animals separated from another's, and herds wandered freely over the open range of grasslands. At the roundup, cowboys traveled through the range, looking for cattle owned by their employers. A cowboy could identify his boss's animals by their brands, distinctive letters or designs that represented a specific ranch. Using a red-hot iron, cowboys burned these images into the hides of their employer's cattle so no other ranch could claim them. During roundups, cowboys also branded recently born calves and kept records on adult animals that were ready to be driven north for sale.

Cattle drives began in the spring, and the herds sometimes numbered in the hundreds, sometimes in the thousands. For a big drive, 10 to 15 cowboys were needed to keep the herd

PICTURING THE WEST

Many elements of the American cowboy's way of life were borrowed from Mexican ranch hands known as *vaqueros*. First taught to ride horses and handle cattle by Spanish conquistadors and missionaries, the vaqueros developed techniques for ranching that included using lassos and letting cattle roam free until the annual roundup. During the nineteenth century, American cowboys adopted many of these techniques as their own. They also began wearing chaps, ponchos, bandannas, and other clothing favored by the vaqueros. Such terms as *bronco*, *buckaroo*, *stampede*, and *rodeo*—all based on Spanish words—further show the vaqueros' lasting influence in the West.

California Vaqueros by James Walker, around 1876

together. Often they traveled the Chisholm Trail, a path that connected north Texas to Abilene, Kansas. Similarly well-worn trails could take them to other cow towns, such as Dodge City and Wichita in Kansas and Denver in Colorado.

On a drive, a few cowboys rode in front of the herd, a few at the side, and a few at the back. Those at the back had the toughest job because they had to constantly be on the lookout for dogies—the cowboy name for orphaned calves who, with no mother to guide them, tended to wander away from the herd. Dirt kicked up by the herd also spelled trouble for riders in the rear. Dust coated their faces and left them coughing for hours.

Cowboy life was full of other discomforts. Each morning cowboys had to be up before dawn. After a big breakfast of beans, beef, bread, and thick coffee, they mounted their horses and began guiding the herd. The cattle moved slowly, stopping often to graze. On an average day, cowboys could cover only about ten miles before camping for the night around the campfire. They slept on the ground covered only by a thin tarp that gave them no protection from wind or rain. A few cowboys assigned to night duty stayed awake all night, watching the herds and protecting them from wolves and other wild animals. To keep the cattle calm and their own eyes open, cowboys on night duty often sang songs about the open range and the loneliness they felt away from home and family.

Though the routine could get dull, cowboys preferred the boredom of the drive to the occasional excitement of storms. Out on the nearly treeless Plains, there was nowhere to hide from pounding rains and lightning. Stampedes were another constant threat because even the slightest noise could panic the herd and set the cattle running wildly. Once a stampede began, a cowboy had to be careful to stay on his horse or else he could be trampled to death.

An African-American cowboy

The Becker sisters, branding cattle on their Colorado ranch in 1894

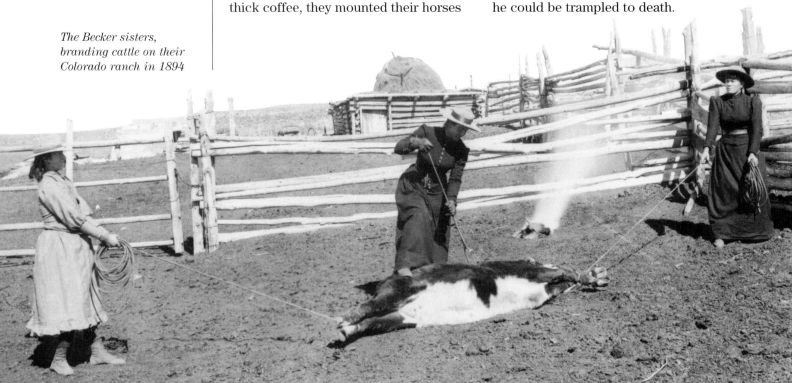

The Great Die-up

When the cattle drives began in the late 1860s, cowboys often had little company besides one another and their cattle. Soon, though, they found themselves sharing the range with others looking to make a living off the land. Like the cattlemen, sheepherders from the Southwest discovered that their animals could thrive on the grassy Plains. Woollies, as the cowboys called the sheep, ate the grass so low that many grazing areas were ruined for cattle. Predictably, cowboys resented the sheepherders and sometimes resorted to violence to drive them from the range.

Also competing with the cowboys for land were pioneer farmers, who fenced in their fields with barbed wire that often injured or even killed cattle that wandered into the fences. The farmers wanted the cowboys to stay away from their land because the cattle frequently carried Texas fever, an animal disease that could kill a farmer's livestock. If an infected herd was driven too close to a farm, all the farm's animals would sicken and die.

Photographed in 1885, these angry masked homesteaders are cutting wire fences built by Nebraska cattlemen.

The Johnson County War

In 1892 the powerful owners of big ranches in Johnson County, Wyoming, were determined to do anything to stay in business—even kill. To get rid of their competition, they hired 46 gunmen from Texas to murder the county's small ranch owners. Among the first victims were rancher Nathan Champion and cattlewoman Ella "Cattle Kate" Watson. Terrified by the killings, the small ranchers formed an army of their own.

Their two-hundred-man posse had the hired gunmen surrounded when U.S. soldiers rode into town to stop the violence.

After the Johnson County War, the gunmen were put on trial for Champion's murder. No one, however, came forward to testify against them. The only witnesses had been kidnapped by friends of the gunmen so they could not appear in court. For lack of evidence, the Johnson County killers were set free.

The blizzard of 1887 left the northern Plains littered with the bodies of frozen dead cattle.

Increasingly, too, cowboys found themselves sharing the range with other cowboys. By the early 1880s news of how much money could be made in the cattle business had brought more investors to Texas. Many came from as far away as England and Scotland, and as the number of cattlemen grew, so did the size of the herds. The owner of the huge King Ranch in southern Texas, for instance, had more than 65,000 cattle. Soon there were far more animals feeding on the range than the land could support, and ranching had spread into the northern Plains—Colorado, Wyoming, Montana, and the Dakotas.

In the winter of 1887, the greed of the cattlemen led to a disaster called the Great Die-up. That January the Plains suffered the worst blizzard ever recorded. Temperatures fell to 68 degrees below zero. It was too cold to drive cattle north.

Cowboys were forced indoors while their cattle were left to brave the snow and bitterly cold winds.

When the spring thaw came, cowboys and cattlemen were horrified by what had happened to their herds. Unable to paw through the mounds of snow to reach the grass beneath, thousands of animals had starved to death. The upper Plains were covered with rotting cattle corpses. Like many cattlemen, rancher Granville Stuart was disgusted by what he saw. He later wrote, "A business that had been fascinating to me before, suddenly became distasteful. I never wanted to own again an animal that I could not feed and shelter."

With much of their herds destroyed, many cattlemen were ruined. Others, realizing that the cattle business was not a sure way to riches, sold their cattle and ranches. Most big ranches closed.

Taking their place were small ranches, whose owners kept their cattle penned and raised hay to make sure that they would not go hungry.

After only about 20 years, the great era of the cowboy was over, though the legacy of the cowboy's way of life remains. Those who wanted to stay in the cattle business had to take jobs as ranch hands, spending their days fixing fences and cutting hay. Even though they had been underpaid and overworked, many sorely missed riding the open range. As former cowboy Edward C. "Teddy Blue" Abbott mournfully wrote, "Just when everything was going fine . . . the whole thing went Ker Plunk, and we are now a prehistoric race."

Western Voices

"Poor old bovines, they would just drift with the storm and bellow until they could go no further; then they'd lie down on the trail and freeze to death. The following spring if a man should ride along any trail, he could count dead cattle by the thousand. . . . The stench from the decomposing cattle was fearful, and one couldn't get away from it."

—cowboy Reuben Mullins, on the fate of the cattle herds during the blizzard of 1887

Lawmen and Outlaws

While the cattle industry was booming, the cow towns prospered as well. Abilene, Dodge City, Wichita, and Denver were filled with stores where cowboys could spend their wages. Their work clothes filthy after completing a cattle drive, many were eager to reward themselves with a new set of duds. Their outfits often included blue denim pants made by Levi Strauss of San Francisco and big hats manufactured by John B. Stetson of Philadelphia. All too often, cowboys spent whatever money they had left at the towns' saloons. In 1870 Abilene had only five hundred permanent residents, but the cowboys who rode into town kept its 32 drinking establishments busy. With these saloons in mind, one visitor called Abilene "the wickedest and most God-forsaken place on the continent."

Guns and liquor indeed proved a lethal combination in the cow towns. Gunfights sometimes erupted. More often, guns went off accidentally in the middle of a brawl. As the towns grew, their residents wanted more protection from casual violence and hired lawmen to police their streets. Some became famous through exaggerated stories of their exploits. Among these legendary lawmen were James "Wild Bill" Hickok,

James "Wild Bill" Hickok was shot and killed while playing poker.

The main street of Dodge City, Kansas, in 1878

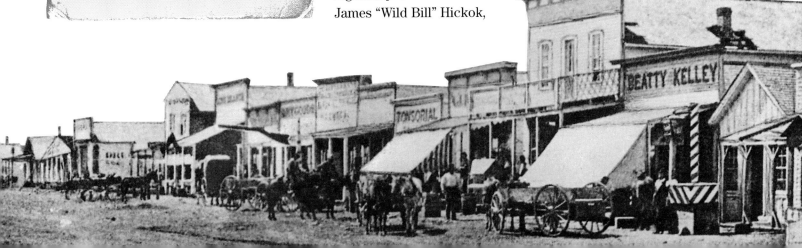

Billy the Kid

Born Henry McCarty in about 1859, Billy the Kid began his life of crime when still a teenager. In New Mexico Territory, he shot his first man, a bully who had been taunting him. Nicknamed The Kid because he was young and small, he fled the law and found work under the name William Bonney in Lincoln County. He got caught up in rivalries between cattlemen there and was soon leading a gang of cattle thieves.

For a criminal, The Kid was surprisingly lighthearted and kind. He won many friends among the cowboys of Lincoln County, but not among the cattlemen. They wanted him stopped. Pat Garrett was elected sheriff by promising to do just that. Garrett broke up the gang and arrested The Kid. After killing two deputies, The Kid escaped, but Garrett tracked him down again. When the sheriff found Billy the Kid, as he was then known, Garrett killed him with a single shot. Almost immediately Billy the Kid became part of American folklore, both admired and scorned for his short, violent life.

sheriff of Abilene, and Wyatt Earp, marshal of Dodge City.

One of the most famous stories in western history occurred in Tombstone, Arizona, a mining boomtown. Earp moved there in 1879 to be with his brothers Virgil and Morgan, and the Earps became respected citizens of Tombstone. A feud developed between them and the Clanton and McLaury brothers, outlaws who regularly harassed the townspeople. To settle a personal score and protect their business interests, the Earps, with the help of Wyatt's friend Doc Holliday, faced down their enemies at the nearby O. K. Corral on October 26, 1881. After a few seconds of shooting, one of the Clantons and two of the McLaurys lay dead; the surviving Clanton brother fled town. Ever since, Wyatt Earp has been celebrated as a man willing to risk his life to restore law and order.

Equally famous in their day were gangs who made their living robbing stagecoaches, trains, and banks. Outlaws such as Black Bart, Belle Starr, the Dalton Brothers, and Butch Cassidy and the Sundance Kid all became part of western lore. The best-known western outlaws, though, were Frank and Jesse James—brothers as daring as they were brutal. Tales of their crimes were particularly exciting. One story claimed that the Jameses boldly robbed a town's bank while a political rally was going on outside. Instead of making a quick getaway, Jesse rode up to the crowd and calmly announced that there seemed to be something strange going on at the bank, before racing away.

The public soon warmed to the James boys even though they were vicious killers and thieves. Largely untrue stories spread that they had turned to crime only after a railroad

company pushed them off their land. They were said to be modern-day Robin Hoods who gave their loot away to the poor. Still, the law dogged the Jameses. After they murdered two men in Missouri in 1881, the state offered five thousand dollars to anyone who killed either of the brothers. Eager to collect the reward, a member of the James gang shot Jesse in his own home in April 1882.

Frank and Jesse James

An engraving of cowboys enjoying themselves in a western saloon

Frank turned himself in and stood trial three times, twice in Missouri and once in Alabama. Each jury, enthralled by his legend, found him not guilty. The lucky Frank gave up crime and lived a quiet life until his death in 1915.

The Populist Revolt

Many owners of small western farms considered the James brothers heroes because the gang's favorite targets—railroads and banks—had become the farmers' own worst enemies by the late nineteenth century. When they first came west, these farmers believed that if they worked hard, they would be able to carve out comfortable lives for themselves and their families. Instead, many had little to show for their labor but a mound of debt. It was difficult to run a successful farm. Even the hardest-working farmer could fail, often because of forces outside his control. Just one year of low rainfall or a sudden drop in the price of corn could mean ruin.

Seeking something to blame for their troubles, angry farmers often focused on railroads. They resented the high rates rail companies charged to transport their crops to market. Many had fury left over for the banks that profited from loans the farmers needed just to stay afloat. Because railroads and banks were largely run by easterners, the farmers saw their problems arising from a battle between East and West—one the West was losing. In their eyes, people in the West seemed to be doing all the work while people in the East seemed to be making all the money.

In the 1870s small farmers started forming organizations so they could help one another protect their interests. The most important of these associations began in Texas and was known as the Farmers' Alliance in Texas. Working together, alliance members tried to pressure the railroads for better rates, keep ranchers from taking over their land, and create their own stores so they would not have to rely on local merchants. Despite its best efforts, the Farmers' Alliance had almost no

BOOMERS AND SOONERS

For much of the nineteenth century, present-day Oklahoma was known as Indian Territory. When the United States pushed eastern Indian tribes off their homelands, the government often sent them to live on reservations there.

But by 1880 good land in the West was becoming scarce, and non-Indians began to eye unsettled areas in Indian Territory, which they wanted for themselves. A few from neighboring Kansas defied the U.S. government by moving onto the land without permission. Soldiers were sent to force the overeager settlers, called Boomers, back over the border; but many refused to stay put. Again and again they slipped into Indian Territory, only to be escorted home by U.S. troops.

The public's hunger for Indian Territory land grew so strong that the government decided to open it to white settlement, regardless of past

promises to the Indian nations that had been settled there. On March 23, 1889, President Benjamin Harrison announced that a two-million-acre area called the Oklahoma District would be opened at noon on April 22. Settlers hoping to make a claim flocked to the district. Troops lined the border to keep out Sooners—impatient settlers who tried to sneak in early.

On the designated day, when the sun was high overhead, the soldiers shot their guns into the air at exactly noon. The "Run," as it was called, was on. Some on horseback, some on bicycle, some on foot, about 100,000 people stormed into the district. All were frantic to find the best plot they could to claim as their own. Within hours, every inch of the Oklahoma District was settled.

Lawyers setting up makeshift offices during the Oklahoma land rush

success. It did, however, help many desperate farmers. Alone on their isolated farms, they felt powerless. But as part of the alliance, they regained a sense of control over their lives. The Farmers' Alliance soon spread throughout the West, and its membership grew to hundreds of thousands.

By 1892 the Farmers' Alliance had become a full-fledged political party. It demanded that the U.S. government take over the country's transportation system and open land granted to the railroads for settlement by homesteaders. It was renamed the People's Party; its members became known as Populists, and their message was called Populism. The spread of Populism was furthered by the party's passionate and colorful leaders, such as Kansan Jerry Simpson. When a political opponent said Simpson was too poor and unsophisticated to wear socks, Simpson turned the insult into a boast, winning the support of many hard-up farmers by proudly calling himself "Sockless Jerry." Another Populist leader was Texan Mary Elizabeth Lease, whose fiery speeches helped

Populist group in Kansas in the 1890s

bring many women into the movement. In one, she blamed the eastern investors working on New York City's Wall Street for all the farmers' problems. "Wall Street owns the country," she declared. "It is no longer a government of the people, for the people, by the people, but a government of Wall Street, for Wall Street, and by Wall Street."

In the 1892 presidential election, the People's Party nominated James B. Weaver from Iowa. Weaver received only one million votes, but the party continued to grow. When many more westerners fell on hard times during an economic downturn in 1893, large numbers embraced Populism and its promise to help the common man.

Despite its popularity, the Populist movement was short-lived. In 1896 its leaders decided to support William

Western Voices

"[T]he great cities rest upon our broad and fertile prairies. Burn down your cities and leave our farms, and your cities will spring up again as if by magic; but destroy our farms and the grass will grow in the streets of every city in the country."

—*presidential candidate William Jennings Bryan, speaking in 1896 on eastern cities' dependence on western farms*

The Last Queen of Hawaii

On August 12, 1898, the westernmost American border was extended thousands of miles, far into the Pacific Ocean, when the island chain of Hawaii was formally transferred to the United States. Hawaii had been an independent country, ruled by kings and queens. But in the 1880s American sugar planters there decided they wanted to take over the islands. They formed an army and pressured Hawaii's King Kalakaua to give them informal control over his government. Wanting to avoid bloodshed at all costs, Kalakaua agreed.

After his death in 1891, his sister Liliuokalani became queen. But when the sugar planters' army marched on the palace in 1893, she too surrendered.

The American planters wanted the United States to annex Hawaii, but President Grover Cleveland refused. Like many other Americans, he believed that what the planters had done was wrong. Cleveland left office in 1896, however, and the new president, William McKinley, had no such qualms. With his support, the United States annexed Hawaii two years later.

Jennings Bryan—the presidential candidate of the Democratic Party—instead of nominating one of their own. Although most westerners voted for Bryan, he lost badly. The East, where the majority of Americans still lived, had thrown its support to the Republican nominee, William McKinley. This bitter defeat spelled the end of Populism, though the suspicion of big business it inspired in many westerners lived on.

Killing the Indian

Kill the Indian and save the man" was the motto of educator Richard Henry Pratt. He was not actually urging the murder of Indian people, but he wanted to "kill" the Indian way of life. His mission was to "save" Indians by persuading them to give up their old customs and live like whites. His views were shared by other reformers who called themselves Friends of the Indian, mostly wealthy people who sincerely wanted to help poor reservation Indians. Despite their good intentions, though, most had little respect for Indians and Indian ways. Instead of asking Indians what they needed, the Friends of the Indian arrogantly assumed they knew what was best for them.

Pratt was convinced that schools were the best way of "saving" the Indian. Although adult Indians might not willingly adopt white ways, children—if taken away from their parents—could be more easily molded. Guided by this idea, in 1879 Pratt founded the Carlisle Indian Industrial School in Carlisle, Pennsylvania.

Most of Carlisle's students came from the Great Plains. They were taken from their homes and families and traveled thousands of miles by train to reach the boarding school. Once there, they were assigned American names and forbidden to speak their own language. Because most did not know English, this rule really meant that if they spoke at all they would be punished, often with a beating. The students had to eat unfamiliar non-Indian foods. They were forced to wear non-Indian suits and dresses that, unlike their traditional clothes, felt hot and scratchy. Some were so miserable and lonely that they tried to run away. Others never got the chance. Exposed for the first time to non-Indian diseases such as measles, many students became sick. Student Luther Standing Bear later remembered that "[within] three years nearly one half of the children from the Plains were dead and through with all earthly schools."

Those who survived spent long days in the classroom. In the morning they were instructed in English, mathematics, and science. In the afternoon boys learned carpentry, tinsmithing, and blacksmithing, while girls learned cooking, sewing, and housekeeping. As part of their lessons, teachers taught them to hate Indian traditions and beliefs. Not surprisingly, after years at Carlisle, many students found it difficult to go home. Because of their schooling, they looked down on the way their families and friends lived. In turn, the relatives of former students sometimes judged them harshly for adopting white customs. Many Carlisle students felt lost, uncomfortable among Indians and non-Indians alike.

In addition to reeducating Indian children, white reformers were determined to turn western Indian hunters into farmers. The Friends of the

Indian assumed that if these Indians took up farming, they would give up their old ways and live just like their white neighbors. The plan, though, made little practical sense. Most western Indians did not have the fertile land, supplies, or know-how to be successful farmers. More important, many of them— particularly Indian men on the Plains— had no interest in this type of work and thought farming was a humiliating way to make a living. In their eyes, to be a man was to be a buffalo hunter.

However, to the Plains Indians' sorrow, the days of the buffalo hunter were over. The situation left many reservation Indians feeling hopeless. They found comfort in a new Indian religion preached by Wovoka, a Northern Paiute Indian holy man who told his followers that one day in early 1889 he had fallen dead while chopping wood. Before coming back to life, he went to heaven. There God spoke to Wovoka, telling him that all Indians should live in peace and dance the traditional Paiute Round Dance.

Rumors about the holy man and his mighty vision began to spread. The next summer a group of Lakota Sioux went to visit him. Excited by his message, they created their own version of his teachings, which became known as the Ghost Dance religion. The Ghost Dance promised that if Indians performed certain ceremonies, their ancestors would come back to life. At the same time, all whites on earth would die. Soon the Ghost Dance spread to other Plains tribes, including the Arapaho and Cheyenne.

When they heard about the Ghost Dance, nearby white settlers were frightened. They worried that the Indians might try to make their dream of a world

without whites come true by killing them. After the panicked settlers demanded that the government do something to

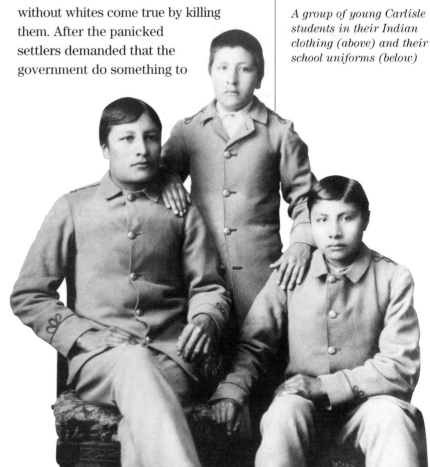

A group of young Carlisle students in their Indian clothing (above) and their school uniforms (below)

The Carlisle Indians

In 1893 40 boys at Carlisle Indian school met with the school's founder, Richard Henry Pratt, to make a special request: They wanted to play football. Pratt agreed under two conditions: "Never slug," he told them, "for you will be judged as savages, and work until you can whip the biggest team in the country."

For the next 20 years the school's team, called the Carlisle Indians, was a football powerhouse. Carlisle's players were driven hard by their coach, Glenn "Pop" Warner. He said the team was "about as perfect a football machine as I ever sent on the field." The members became famous for their trick plays. In a 1903 game against Harvard, they invented the hidden ball trick, in which a Carlisle guard stuffed the ball under his shirt and ran for a touchdown before the other team could figure out where the ball was.

Carlisle's greatest player was Jim Thorpe. A member of the Sauk and Fox Nation in Oklahoma, he won two gold medals at the 1912 Olympics and then had a career in both professional baseball and football.

A mass grave for victims of the Wounded Knee Massacre

stop the Ghost Dance, hundreds of U.S. troops were sent out to restore order on the Plains.

By this time the Lakota leader Sitting Bull was living on Standing Rock Reservation in North Dakota. He did not strongly support the Ghost Dance, but because many whites were convinced that the great warrior would lead the Ghost Dancers to revolt, the government's agent at Standing Rock demanded his arrest. On December 15, 1890, reservation police stormed Sitting Bull's house, as a crowd of angry Lakota followers gathered outside. In the tense atmosphere, a gunfight broke out. Six policemen and eight Lakota—Sitting Bull among them—were dead.

The Ghost Dancers had no desire to fight the U.S. army. To show they wanted

to live in peace, their leaders decided they should move their camps closer to the agent's headquarters on Pine Ridge Reservation in South Dakota. There the agent could watch them and see that they wanted no trouble.

While traveling to the agency, one group of about 350 Ghost Dancers, led by the elderly and ill chief Big Foot, camped along Wounded Knee Creek. On December 29, U.S. troops confronted them and demanded they surrender their weapons. The soldiers treated the Indians roughly and grabbed at their guns. One went off, probably accidentally. The sound, though, convinced the troops that they had a battle on their hands and they shot into the crowd of Indians. The survivors fled for the woods, with the soldiers on their heels. The troops shot at everyone, including old people and children, not caring whether or not they were armed. Before the Wounded Knee Massacre was over, more than three hundred people had been killed.

The Wild West

By the end of the nineteenth century, the West was different from the place it had been only decades before. The buffalo herds that had blanketed the Plains were dead. Once-proud Indian warriors and hunters were confined to reservations, dependent on government rations for their survival. And the cowboys—the onetime kings of the open range—were now menial workers, forced to spend their days fencing in the lands where they used to roam freely. The Old West, it seemed, was gone forever, except in one place— a traveling show called Buffalo Bill's Wild West. Beginning in 1883, it entertained millions of people, touring cities throughout the eastern United States and Europe.

Wherever Buffalo Bill's Wild West was due to arrive, the advertising men— sometimes three train cars full—plastered walls, fences, and any other surface they could find with thousands of colorful posters, announcing that the greatest spectacle on earth was coming to town. A gleaming white, 26-car train then rolled into the station. Crews of strong men hopped out carrying enormous canvas tents and tall electric lamps that soon transformed an empty patch of land into a fabulous arena drenched with light even late into the night.

"A Host of Western Celebrities; A Camp of Cheyenne, Arapahoe, Sioux and Pawnee Indians; A Group of Mexican Vaqueros; Round-up of Western Cow-Boys; . . . A Herd of Wild Buffalos; A Corral of Indian Ponies; . . . Mountain Lions, Coyottes, Deer, Antelope, Mountain Sheep, etc."

—*from an 1886 program for Buffalo Bill's Wild West*

A poster advertising Buffalo Bill's Wild West

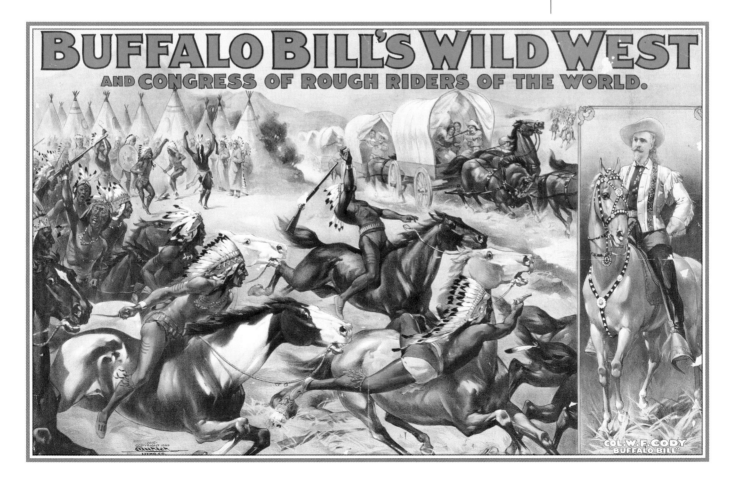

*William "Buffalo Bill" Cody
leading a procession of his
Indian performers in a 1907
publicity photo*

On the day of the show, the arena teemed with people—including hundreds of performers and many more ticket-buyers eager to see the thrilling sights the advertising posters promised. Few left disappointed. During the three-hour program, Indians raced by the audience mounted on mighty steeds and wearing feathered warbonnets so long they dragged on the ground behind them. Cowboys astonished the crowd with their sharpshooting and skill at riding wild, bucking horses. Perhaps most exciting were the reenactments of dramatic western scenes, including a stagecoach robbery, a buffalo hunt, and an Indian attack on a homesteader's cabin.

The show was the invention of William F. Cody, who called himself Buffalo Bill onstage. Born in 1846, Cody had traveled the West as a young man and worked just about any job he could find. He was a fur trapper, buffalo hunter,

stagecoach driver, Pony Express rider, scout for the U.S. army, and guide for travelers from the East. His greatest talent, though, was as a performer. His career in entertainment started when he met Edward Judson, a writer from New York State who wrote cheap storybooks called dime novels under the name Ned Buntline. Judson thought the flamboyant Cody would make the ideal hero for his stories about the West. He talked to Cody about his many adventures and then wrote wildly exaggerated versions of them in his books.

Soon Cody was asked to play himself onstage, acting out the stories Buntline had written about him. Cody loved the cheers of the audience almost as much as the money he made. To make even more, he decided to stage a show of his own. Bold and often reckless, Cody imagined an extravaganza too big for any stage. His show would feature a cast of hundreds performing in the open air.

"The Romantic West Brought East in Reality," declared one poster for the show. Although it offered many easterners their first chance to see the Indians, cowboys, and buffalo they had read about in newspapers and books, the pageant was hardly a true picture of the West. The show's dramas told simplistic stories in which good triumphed over evil. In the plays, white frontiersmen like Buffalo Bill were always the heroes and Indians and Mexicans were always the villains. One of the most popular plays depicted the famous Battle of Little Bighorn of 1876. Buffalo Bill's Wild West presented the Indians as bloodythirsty savages. But the Indian actors playing these parts knew that in real life the warriors were only trying to protect their territory and families from the soldiers invading their lands.

Despite the show's unflattering view of Indians, many young Indian men, mostly Lakota Sioux, were eager to work for Cody. On their reservations they were bored and often hungry. Working in the show gave them a chance to travel, make a little money, and eat regular meals. Even better, it let them show off their skill with horses and rifles. If they could no longer be real hunters and warriors on the Plains, onstage they could at least pretend they were.

For 30 years Buffalo Bill's Wild West was one of America's favorite entertainments. But eventually audiences grew tired of the show and stopped coming. Bankrupt, Cody was forced to take down his tents for the last time in 1913. His Wild West, however, would live on in a new type of show—the movie western. For many years to come, the myths Cody staged would again be presented onscreen as the real West.

LITTLE SURE SHOT

Buffalo Bill's greatest star was a slight young woman named Annie Oakley, who had earned a reputation as an expert trick shooter while still a teenager in Ohio. There she beat Frank Butler, a professional marksman, in a shooting competition. Impressed by Annie and her talent, Butler courted and married her.

At only twenty-five Oakley was asked to join Buffalo Bill's show. She was billed as "Little Sure Shot"—a nickname given to her by the great Lakota Sioux chief Sitting Bull, who costarred with her in the show. She amazed her audiences by cutting a playing card in two with a series of shots and by shooting an apple off the head of her little poodle, George. Onstage, she wore a costume she designed herself, featuring a shirt covered with jewels and medals and a huge white cowboy hat.

Buffalo Bill's Wild West made Oakley a celebrity around the world. When the show was in France, the crowd shouted her name and yelled wildly as she raced across the arena on horseback, using three rifles to shatter six glass balls thrown high in the air. Women all over Paris gave up their fancy gowns to wear cowgirl outfits like Annie's.

PICTURING THE WEST

At 5:12 A.M. on April 18, 1906, one of the worst earthquakes of all time rocked the city of San Francisco, California. Lasting less than a minute, the quake caused substantial destruction; but even worse were the fires that it ignited. For three days fire ripped through the city, leveling 28,000 buildings and leaving 225,000 people homeless—more than half of San Francisco's population. At the time, about seven hundred deaths were attributed to the quake, although more recent research suggests the actual number may have been closer to three thousand.

Dakota (1903). In 1908 Roosevelt also declared the Grand Canyon in present-day Arizona a national park.

With their shared passion for the outdoors, Roosevelt and John Muir became friends. Their views of how humans fit into nature, though, were very different. Muir believed in preservation—that people should leave as much of the wilderness untouched as possible. Roosevelt believed in conservation—that people should treat the land carefully so that it could be used for generations to come. In fact, Roosevelt thought humans had a duty to make use of nature and its products. He agreed with Pinchot, who said that "wilderness is waste."

With this idea in mind, conservationists at the Forest Service did not try to keep loggers out of the national forests. Instead, they made rules specifying who could use the forests and how the trees could be harvested. Similarly, the National Park Service did not leave parklands unchanged. They built roads and trails and encouraged businesspeople to

establish nearby hotels, restaurants, and shops. The conservationists considered these changes improvements that would keep tourists comfortable as they toured the parks.

Their creators believed that the carefully laid out national parks had another use: They were great "earth monuments" to American culture. Whereas Europeans could celebrate their nations by pointing to the grand art and architecture their people had produced over centuries, the United States was just a young country, still less than 150 years old. Though it had few human-made monuments to rival those of Europe, it did have the beautiful and timeless scenic vistas of the West.

In 1901 the conservationists and preservationists found themselves in a battle over the Hetch Hetchy Valley in Yosemite National Park. Due west of San Francisco, the area, in John Muir's words, was "one of Nature's rarest and most precious mountain temples." It also contained precious water that the city's population needed. Prominent San Franciscans petitioned to dam the

The Harvey Girls

In the early twentieth century advertisements ran in newspapers throughout the United States inviting young women to become Harvey Girls—the nickname given to waitresses hired by the Fred Harvey Company, which operated restaurants and hotels along the Santa Fe railroad line. The work was long and hard. Not only were Harvey Girls on duty all day seven days a week, they also had to be careful not to break any of Fred Harvey's many rules. The women had to be polite at all times, keep their uniforms sparkling clean, and promise not to marry while they worked for the company. Despite these demands, about 100,000 women signed on as Harvey Girls. Some welcomed the chance to leave home and live on their own in an era when few jobs were open to women. Others just wanted a little adventure out west before settling down.

Women in their Harvey Girl uniforms

A small farm in the Dust Bowl during a dust storm

Tuolumne River, which would drench the beautiful valley; Muir and his supporters strongly opposed the damming of the Tuolumne. But the people of San Francisco fought equally hard to get more water, and their demands grew even louder when much of the city was destroyed by fire after a 1906 earthquake. In 1913 they finally won the battle, and the dam was built. The next year, the disheartened Muir died, knowing his beloved Hetch Hetchy had disappeared under a sea of water.

The Dust Bowl

During the early twentieth century dams were built on rivers throughout the West. In 1902 Congress passed the Reclamation Act, which allowed the government to use money it received from selling western land to fund these projects. Dams enabled people to control nature's water supply better. Without dams, big western cities like San Francisco and Los Angeles would not have had enough water for their growing populations.

The Reclamation Act also recognized a bitter truth that many westerners had already learned the hard way: Much of western land was very dry—too dry to farm without irrigation. By 1900 large numbers of hopeful homesteaders who had come to the Plains in the previous century had given up, because their land was not rich or wet enough for successful farming. Those who stayed found they had to work harder to stay ahead. Many kept expanding the size of their farms, relying on bank loans for the money to

"[Sometimes a dust] cloud is seen to be approaching from a distance of many miles. . . . [I]t hangs low, seeming to hug the earth . . . As it sweeps onward, the landscape is progressively blotted out. Birds fly in terror before the storm, and only those that are strong of wing may escape. The smaller birds fly until they are exhausted, then fall to the ground, to share the fate of the thousands of jack rabbits which perish from suffocation."

—Kansas farmer Lawrence Svobida, writing in 1968 about a dust cloud he saw in the 1930s

buy supplies; to pay off the loans, they had to plow and maintain more and more land.

Beginning in 1931, the Plains farmers faced still another problem—drought. For the next ten years, the rainfall on the Plains was far lower than normal. And without enough rainwater, the farmers' crops shriveled and died. The situation was the worst on the southern Plains, where farmers had plowed up much of the grasses that grew there naturally. After their crops failed to grow, the plowed plots became huge patches of loose dirt. Whenever winds blew up, they carried the dirt into the air, forming great clouds of dust. The dust clouds were often so dense that they blackened the sky, and farmers had to stay indoors because breathing the dust could be deadly. Many cattle died when their lungs filled with dirt.

The worst dust storm happened on April 14, 1935, a day that became known as Black Sunday. This single storm blew up more than 300 million tons of dirt; the intense winds carried the dust hundreds of miles east. Dirt from the Plains fell on the streets of New York City and even on boats far out in the Atlantic Ocean. The great dust storms gave a new name to the farmlands in western Kansas, Oklahoma, Texas, eastern Colorado, and New Mexico— the Dust Bowl.

The drought that created the Dust Bowl could not have come at a worse time. During the 1930s the United States was suffering from the Great Depression, a worldwide economic crisis that left millions of

Black Gold

In the late nineteenth century drilling for oil in Texas was a risky venture. Businessmen known as wildcatters spent huge sums trying to tap pools of oil hidden hundreds of feet under the ground. Figuring out where to drill was a guessing game—one that most wildcatters lost.

One winner was Anthony F. Lucas. An engineer, Lucas leased six hundred acres of land near Beaumont, Texas, in 1899. After two years of drilling, oil began to sputter from Lucas's oil well, called Spindletop, on January 10, 1901. The oil was under so much pressure that within moments it began flying out of the ground, rising more than two hundred feet into the air. Crowds gathered to watch the gusher. Before workers brought the flow under control six days later, Spindletop had spewed out more than a half million gallons of oil, creating a sticky black lake.

News of Spindletop brought thousands of would-be oilmen to Texas, all hoping to strike it rich in black gold, as oil was nicknamed.

Like this traveler, heading west on foot, thousands of farmers fled the Dust Bowl, hoping to find a better life in California.

DOROTHEA LANGE: PHOTOGRAPHER

A desperate woman, her forehead wrinkled with concern, looks into the distance as her children clutch her side, clinging to their mother as if she were their only hope. This *Migrant Mother*, taken by Dorothea Lange, is one of the most famous American photographs of the 1930s.

Lange began her career in the 1920s in San Francisco by taking portraits of the city's wealthiest citizens. After ten years, she realized she wanted to photograph not just the rich, but "all kinds of people, people who paid me and people who didn't."

Soon she was turning her camera on the homeless and unemployed who flocked to California in search of paying work. From 1935 to 1941, Lange worked for the government in the Farm Security Administration (FSA). The FSA used her pictures to illustrate reports on how Americans were coping with the Depression.

Simple and direct, Lange's images told the public much more about people's suffering than statistics could. They helped rally support for the government's New Deal programs designed to help the poor. Through her work, Lange fulfilled her life's mission—in her own words, "to make a place where . . . what I did would count."

people out of work. To help the poor and jobless throughout the country, President Franklin D. Roosevelt created a series of policies called the New Deal. A few New Deal programs aided many ranchers and farm owners of the Dust Bowl, though these efforts did little to help the most impoverished people in the area—tenant farmers, who worked land owned by someone else. During the Depression, many landowners evicted tenant farm families from their land.

New Deal programs helped the landlords buy tractors. With these machines, they could make more money farming their land themselves than having tenant farmers do the work.

The situation was a disaster for the tenant farmers, who could barely make ends meet in the best of times. In the worst of times, like the Depression, they faced starvation.

With no land or jobs available, many people had no choice but to leave their farms. The families who fled the Dust Bowl became known as Okies. The nickname was short for "Oklahoma," though many Okies came from other Dust Bowl states. The Okies packed what little they had into old trucks and headed west on Route 66, a road that took them straight to southern California, where they hoped to find better opportunities. With its warm climate and rich farmland, California seemed like a paradise.

Many found their hopes dashed as soon as they arrived there. Because paying work was already scarce, most Californians did not want these poor farmers in their state, competing for the few jobs available. In 1936 the police chief of Los Angeles even ordered officers to stand along the state border, forming a "bum blockade" to keep the Okies out.

However unwelcome, about 750,000 Dust Bowl emigrants found a new home in California. Many settled in Los Angeles, where they took jobs as factory workers and low-paid laborers. Others earned meager wages picking fruits and vegetables on nearby farms. These migrant farmworkers were so poor that they had to live in filthy makeshift camps set up in irrigation ditches. In his novel *The Grapes of Wrath*, John Steinbeck wrote about these horrible living conditions while telling the story of the Joads, a Dust Bowl family turned California fruit pickers. Partly because of Steinbeck's book, the Dust Bowl farmworkers became a symbol of the misery felt by millions of poor Americans during the 1930s.

The War Years

On the morning of December 7, 1941, Japanese planes flew over the Hawaiian island of Oahu, dropping bombs on the U.S. army base at Pearl Harbor below. Within days Congress had declared war on Japan and its German and Italian allies. The United States was now in the thick of the great conflict known as World War II.

Wartime workers at a California shipyard shown in a photo by Dorothea Lange

The Zoot Suit Riots

During the war years, old tensions between whites and Mexican Americans in Los Angeles grew even stronger. The police and press were largely to blame, branding all Mexican-American men as criminals because of the actions of a few gang members. As a result, whites in the city regularly insulted and harassed Mexican Americans they met on city streets.

The anger between the two groups erupted into violence in early June 1943. For a week groups of white men, mostly soldiers, roamed through the city, beating and stripping the clothing off Mexican Americans dressed in zoot suits—jackets with wildly exaggerated shoulders, pants with wide legs, and enormous hats. Zoot suits were a craze that the white rioters seemed to associate with Mexican-American gangs; but in fact, most zoot suiters were teenagers, who dressed this way to rebel against their parents.

A zoot suiter

The attack on Pearl Harbor frightened people living along the Pacific Ocean. Afraid of a full-scale invasion by the Japanese, some left the coast, moving inland for the duration of the war. Many others, however, headed to the coast, where almost overnight factories began sprouting up, especially in the cities and towns along the Pacific. In these factories laborers made the airplanes and ships the U.S. military needed for its war effort.

The U.S. government poured billions of dollars into businesses producing wartime goods. About 10 percent of this money was spent in California, where Los Angeles, San Francisco, and San Diego became centers for building war machines. Other important factories included Boeing Aircraft in Seattle, Washington, and the Kaiser shipyard in Portland, Oregon.

The Great Plains also prospered because of the wartime demand for food products. As luck would have it, the ten-year drought that had made the southern Plains into the Dust Bowl had just ended. Farmers, sure their hard times were over, began plowing as much land as they could to cash in on rising crop prices.

As factories and farms expanded, the poverty of the Depression years ended. Instead of too many workers and not enough jobs, there were now too many jobs and not enough workers. So much war work was available in the West that many easterners flooded into the area. During the war some eight million Americans from east of the Mississippi moved to lands west of the river.

Because most able-bodied American men were in the military, companies had to search actively for people to hire. The seven Kaiser shipyards in Washington, Oregon, and California, which had built nearly 1,500 ships for the U.S. miltary during the war, sent recruiters to the Plains to find potential workers. They offered high salaries and good housing to lure employees. Many factories found the workers they needed by hiring women for jobs that previously had been considered "man's work." The companies told them it was their patriotic duty to take wartime jobs, but many women found the good pay of factory work was all the encouragement they needed to sign on. In the aircraft industry in Los Angeles, nearly half of the wartime workers were women.

The need for labor also led some western companies to hire African Americans for the first time. Many African Americans, particularly those living in the South, were eager to move west to take advantage of these wartime jobs. One African-American job applicant at an aircraft plant making B-17 bombers later remembered, "Man, I didn't know what . . . a B-17 was, but I wanted to learn, I wanted an opportunity."

African-American job seekers were just as happy to escape the strong prejudices of many white southerners. Though they were generally treated better in western cities—especially in Los Angeles and Oakland, California— they still encountered racism. Whites often refused to let African Americans

patronize many hotels and restaurants or live in certain neighborhoods, and African-American children were even turned away from parks.

White business owners were less willing to overcome their prejudices against Mexicans, who were usually hired only for work on farms—back-breaking, low-paying jobs that no one else wanted. Farm owners were so desperate for labor that they tried to recruit even more workers from Mexico. But the Mexican government was so appalled by the laborers' low wages and poor working conditions that it stepped in to stop them. Only when the United States negotiated a minimum pay rate for Mexicans were more allowed to immigrate north. Under this program, about 200,000 Mexican workers—called *braceros*—were employed on western farms during the war. Despite the United States' guarantees, many were treated terribly by their employers.

The Japanese Americans of California were the victims of even more brutal racism during the war. Two months after the Pearl Harbor attack, President Roosevelt ordered that they be sent to internment camps, where they would be kept separated from the rest of the population. Many whites, convinced that Japanese Americans

Western Voices

"I didn't even have to go for the job; people were coming to me for jobs. Not only just me, but everyone. They were recruiting workers and they didn't care whether you were black, white, young, old. . . . They were begging for workers."

—factory worker Norma Cantrell, on finding wartime jobs in California in 1942

Female factory workers helping to assemble a B-17 warplane

Japanese-American children on their way to an internment camp

Los Alamos and the Atomic Bomb

As a boy, scientist J. Robert Oppenheimer spent a summer on a ranch in northern New Mexico. He never forgot the region's beautiful mountains and nearly empty landscape. When in 1942 he was asked by the government to head a secret project, he decided New Mexico would be the perfect place for it.

Almost overnight, the town of Los Alamos grew up. There, Oppenheimer gathered the best physicists, chemists, engineers, and technicians in the country. Their task was to create an atomic bomb—a weapon far more powerful than any other ever built.

On July 16, 1945, the Los Alamos scientists conducted the first atomic bomb test near Alamogordo, New Mexico. Weeks later, on August 6 and 9, the United States dropped atomic bombs on two Japanese cities— Hiroshima and Nagasaki. The horrible destruction and death caused by the bombs persuaded Japan to surrender, ending World War II.

would try to help Japan win the war, believed that by confining Japanese Americans in camps, U.S. officials could make sure they did not pass along any crucial information to the enemy.

In reality, Japanese Americans posed little threat. When Roosevelt gave his order, no Japanese American had committed any act of espionage against the United States. Also, about two thirds were American citizens, most of whom had never even seen Japan. Still, many officials believed that Japanese Americans would be more loyal to the country of their ancestors than to the country where they were born and raised. This notion, though defying common sense, revealed the long-held prejudice western whites had against Japanese immigrants.

Beginning in 1942, the Japanese Americans on the West Coast were given a few weeks' warning to sell their businesses and homes. They were then sent to ten internment camps, eight of

which were located in desert lands in the West. Although some camp residents were released to work on farms or attend college, most were forced to stay for years. In 1944 the U.S. Supreme

Western Voices

"[T]he army came and said within two weeks, pack a suitcase and one duffle bag and be at this railroad siding twelve o'clock sharp. . . . [T]hey didn't tell us how long we'd be gone or when we could expect to get back. . . . I lived in a little community of about fifty families. . . . But one day we were all there, and the next day at noon they were gone, no Japanese Americans left in this town."

—*Japanese-American Seichi Hayashida, on being sent to an internment camp*

Court finally ruled that the internment camps violated the U.S. Constitution because the Japanese Americans being held had done nothing wrong. Over the next two years, the camps were disbanded. Some Japanese Americans refused to return to the West; most of them moved to eastern states, and a few went to live in Japan. Those who returned to the Pacific coast had to start their lives over. Their houses, their businesses, their neighborhoods—all had been lost. Perhaps even worse, their white neighbors still treated them like criminals, even though they had committed no crime.

California
Dreams

On August 15, 1945, Japan surrendered to the United States and its allies. Like all other Americans, westerners were thrilled that World War II was over. After their victory celebrations, however, many began worrying about what their future held. Wartime had brought plenty of good

jobs and money into the West. Now that the war was won, they wondered, would they again find themselves out of work?

To their relief, the wartime jobs turned into peacetime jobs. After World War II, the United States feared it was on the brink of still another war—this time with the Soviet Union. To be prepared, it continued to buy planes and ships built in western factories. Sure of factory work, many servicemen returning from the war moved to western cities.

For generations, Americans had seen the West as an ideal place to make a fresh start. These veterans were no different. Those who wanted to start families were especially taken with the region, which offered vast space and clean air and seemed a perfect setting to raise children.

Southern California was the destination for many. Good jobs and sunny weather drew millions of Americans to the Los Angeles area. To accommodate them, the city expanded quickly. But unlike many eastern cities,

The internment camp at Manzanar, California

Hollywood

In the film industry's early years, most movies—even westerns—were filmed in New York and New Jersey. But beginning in 1907, independent producers started moving west, particularly to Los Angeles. There they could work without the interference of large eastern movie companies, which were trying to drive them out of business. Los Angeles also offered sunny, warm weather that allowed them to film outdoors all year.

In 1911 the first movie crew came to Hollywood, then a small Los Angeles neighborhood. Living quietly among citrus and avocado groves, its four thousand residents took pride in their reputation for respectability. They quickly tired of unruly movie people disturbing their peaceful community. The crews set up their cameras wherever they wanted, often tying up traffic shooting street scenes. Soon Hollywood apartment houses began posting signs reading, NO DOGS AND ACTORS ALLOWED.

In just a few years Hollywood became the center of the American film industry. By the mid-1920s movies had become California's most profitable industry.

By the 1950s many western highways were already crowded with traffic.

Los Angeles grew outward, not upward. Instead of crowding into downtown skyscrapers, Los Angeles's new residents wanted to live outside the city's center. In outlying neighborhoods called suburbs, they could have comfortable new houses with large lawns where their children could play in the open air.

To satisfy the huge demand for suburban homes, builders in California devised the subdivision—a tract of land, divided into smaller plots, one for each house. Once the plan for the subdivision was made, teams of construction workers built the houses on a strict schedule. Within weeks, where bean fields or fruit orchards had once stood was a complete neighborhood, covered with identical-looking new homes. The favorite house design was the ranch, a one-story house with big windows that allowed people to see the outdoors from the air-conditioned interior.

Americans all over the country were soon clamoring to move into subdivisions and ranch houses. Even if they

Newly built homes in Los Angeles, 1947

DISNEYLAND

To all who come to this happy place: welcome. Disneyland is your land. These words, engraved on a plaque, greeted visitors to America's first theme park. Opened in Anaheim, California, on July 17, 1955, Disneyland was the dream of Walt Disney, the animator who had created Mickey Mouse, Donald Duck, and other popular cartoon characters.

Disney envisioned his park as "a place for California to be at home." Born on a Kansas farm, he had moved to Los Angeles in 1923 to seek his fortune. His experiences helped him understand exactly what kind of entertainment Californians wanted—especially those who flocked there after the war seeking the good life. Disney's "land" was clean and staffed with smiling, helpful employees. Its rides and attractions were built for parents and children to enjoy together in the fresh outdoors year-round.

Designed by Hollywood screenwriters, the sections of the

Disneyland on its opening day

park reflected the new Californians' sense of where they came from and where they were going. In Main Street USA, they could visit a version of the small towns they had left behind. In Frontierland, they experienced a vision of the Old West that retained the adventure but removed the violence. And in Tomorrowland they could see new

technological marvels that gave them, in Disney's words, "faith in the future." The combination proved winning not only to Californians, but to all Americans. Using new highways, families from all over the country loaded into cars and flocked to Disneyland, making it the nation's most popular tourist attraction of the 1950s.

lived in the East, they wanted to move to western-style suburbs, such as the planned community of Levittown, New York. Soon, though, people began to see problems with the suburban way of life, particularly in southern California. In old downtown areas, residents used buses, trolleys, or subways to get around. In suburban Los Angeles, however, there was no public transportation; everyone

had to drive a car to get to work or to go shopping. So many roads and parking lots were needed that eventually nearly one third of the Los Angeles area was paved over. Yet even with more roads, traffic was heavy, and cars were often stuck in traffic jams for hours. And with more traffic came smog—a haze caused by car exhaust and other pollutants. Many suburbanites who went west for

ALAN LADD JEAN ARTHUR VAN HEFLIN

GEORGE STEVENS' PRODUCTION OF

SHANE

Color by Technicolor

BRANDON DE WILDE with JACK PALANCE
BEN JOHNSON EDGAR BUCHANAN Produced and Directed by GEORGE STEVENS
Story by A. B. GUTHRIE, JR.   Motion Picture by JACK SHER   JACK SCHAEFER
A PARAMOUNT PICTURE

A poster for the 1953 western movie Shane

Clayton Moore as the Lone Ranger, the hero of a popular television show of the 1950s

the healthy life found themselves spending much of their time stuck in cars surrounded by filthy air.

In addition to the subdivision, Americans of the 1950s and 1960s came to love another Los Angeles invention—the Hollywood western, movies that told heroic stories of the Old West featuring cowboys, ranchers, outlaws, and lawmen and kept the romance of the Old West alive. Ever since the movie industry began in the early twentieth century, westerns had been popular; but in the 20 years after World War II, they became a craze. About one in every four American films made during this period was a western. Although these movies were set in the nineteenth century, they often explored ideas that concerned many Americans. Though some westerns were just simple tales of good guys fighting bad guys, others presented more complicated heroes who struggled to create their own code of honor in a violent world. These characters appealed to many veterans trying to make sense of their own war experiences. Just as they went to the real West to make a new start, war veterans visited the Hollywood West to help find their place in postwar America.

Many Peoples, Many Protests

In mid-twentieth-century westerns the hero could be a cowboy, a sheriff, or even a bandit, but the villain was almost always an Indian. The Indians then living in the West, however, hardly posed a threat to anyone. Most western Indians lived on reservations, largely hidden from view by non-Indian America. While many whites in the West prospered, reservation Indians grew poorer. Many were left jobless and hopeless.

Partly to help reservation Indians, the U.S. government established a policy known as relocation, which encouraged young Indians to move to cities, such as Los Angeles, San Francisco, Denver, and Minneapolis. Relocation officials said they would find good jobs and live in beautiful new homes. To many poor Indians living in broken-down houses with no running water, these promises were exciting. After they agreed to relocate to cities, however, most were disappointed. Untrained and uneducated, few found work. Instead of building better lives in cities, they merely exchanged reservation poverty for urban poverty. Urban Indians were also mistreated by bigoted non-Indians who looked down on them.

In 1968 a group of Indians in Minneapolis decided to fight back and formed an organization called the American Indian Movement (AIM). AIM's first mission was to take on the city's police force, which regularly harassed and beat Indians for no reason. Armed with cameras, AIM members photographed the police actions and called attention to their abuses. AIM's success caused Indians from many different tribes in other cities to join the group. Most were young people whose parents had been relocated. Even though all they had known was city life, they were eager to help the older people still living on reservations.

In 1973 AIM turned its attention to the Lakota Sioux's reservation at Pine Ridge, South Dakota. There tribal police,

Two members of the American Indian Movement stand guard during their 1973 occupation of Wounded Knee

with the support of U.S. officials, were attacking the older, more traditional reservation residents. AIM decided to stage a protest to show what was happening. On February 28, fully armed, they took over Wounded Knee, the site of the U.S. army's massacre of more than three hundred Lakota in 1890. The protest lasted for 71 days and was reported all over the world. Through the Wounded Knee action, young Indians of the West spoke out against the troubles at Pine Ridge and the injustices Indians had suffered throughout American history.

AIM's protest tactics were inspired by the Black Panthers, an African-American organization formed in Oakland, California, in 1966. Dressed in black and armed with automatic weapons, the Panthers staged violent protests and encouraged other African Americans to rise up in revolt. Although the Panthers received plenty of publicity, they did not attract a large membership even though many African-American Californians shared their anger. The 1950s and 1960s had been difficult years for them. Following the war, many white factory owners stopped hiring African Americans. If they could

"History will judge societies and governments—and their institutions— not by how big they are or how well they serve the rich and the powerful, but by how effectively they respond to the needs of the poor and the helpless."

—*United Farm Workers organizer Cesar Chavez in the 1960s*

A poster for a charity event held to benefit the United Farm Workers

find jobs at all, the work was usually low-paying, such as cleaning houses or waiting tables. African-American neighborhoods were overcrowded, because nearly all the new subdivisions and houses built after the war were reserved for whites.

By 1965 the Watts district of Los Angeles— a large African-American neighborhood—was crowded with poor and desperate people. On August 11 a police investigation into a minor car accident there turned into a full-scale riot. Watts residents—angry, frustrated, and tired of white policemen treating them like criminals and of white store owners overcharging them—took to the streets. Some 30,000 rioters burned and looted stores and other buildings. Thirty-four people were killed, hundreds were injured, and at least $40 million in property was destroyed. The Watts riots were the first

of many that erupted in American cities in the late 1960s.

During this period, Mexican Americans in the West also expressed their anger through protests. Many young Mexican Americans started calling themselves Chicanos—a word that whites meant as an insult but that they used as a show of pride. Just as the American Indian Movement united Indians of many tribes, the Chicano movement attracted Chicanos with different backgrounds—from recent emigrants from Mexico to Mexican Americans whose families had lived in the United States for generations. In just one of the many Chicano protests, in 1968, about ten thousand students from five Los Angeles high schools walked out of class, angry at the poor quality of the education they were receiving and at the racist attitudes of many white teachers.

An even more wide-reaching protest movement was led by Cesar Chavez. As a boy, he and his brother were told to leave a California diner by a waitress who said, "We don't sell to Mexicans." Humiliated by the experience, Chavez was determined to fight discrimination against his people. He helped form the United Farm Workers, a union founded to help Mexican-American farm laborers get better wages and working conditions. In 1968 the UFW launched a campaign to stop growers from hiring nonunion workers and asked shoppers not to buy grapes and lettuce, crops harvested largely by Mexican-American farmworkers in California, unless they were marked with a union label. Millions of Americans throughout the country supported the UFW's boycott. Mexican Americans were particularly enthusiastic, seeing the protest as a symbol of their ongoing fight for equality. Writer Richard

Rodriguez remembered that even though his parents worked in downtown Sacramento, they still sent Chavez money to help the farmworkers. "The hardness of his struggle on the land," Rodriguez later wrote, "reminded them of the hardness of their Mexican past."

The New Western Frontier

More than a century ago, at the Chicago World's Fair in 1893, a young scholar from Wisconsin named Frederick Turner delivered a speech in which he said that the first stage of American history was over. Since the country's beginnings, Americans had steadily moved west in search of free land and a better life. Now that the West was filling up with people, Turner declared, "The frontier has gone."

Turner's ideas upset many people. Like him, they believed that the lure of the western frontier had made Americans an energetic people, always confident to meet any new challenge. With the closing of the frontier, they feared Americans would become lazy and the United States would lose its power. But despite Turner's dire predictions, the West has remained a vibrant place that still excites the imagination of the world. Free western land may be a thing of the past, but the West continues to be a place where people seek a new beginning.

In 1965 the United States changed its immigration laws, making it easier for foreigners to enter the country. Since then, a flood of immigrants—from such countries as Mexico, China, the Philippines, India, and the Dominican Republic—have arrived in the West. Many sought a way out of the poverty they knew in their own countries. Others, from nations such as Vietnam and Nicaragua, immigrated to escape war. Most of the new immigrants have flocked to cities, particularly Los Angeles and San Francisco in California and Houston in Texas. In fact, these newcomers have made the population of Los Angeles the most diverse of any city in the world, encompassing people from more than 140 countries, including Mexicans, Filipinos, Koreans, Japanese,

Silicon Valley

In 1951 Stanford University—a leading school for scientists and engineers—launched an experiment of its own. It bulldozed the cherry and apricot orchards on lands it owned in California's Santa Clara Valley to clear the way for the Stanford Industrial Park. In this sprawling complex, Stanford's talented faculty and students worked with electronics companies to make new products.

Over the next 50 years, hundreds of computer and electronics firms moved to the Santa Clara Valley. By the 1980s it had become the center of the exploding personal computer industry. Essential parts of these computers were microchips, which were made using the element silicon. The area soon became known around the globe by a new name—Silicon Valley.

The signs on these shops in California reflect the influx of Asian immigrants.

On a Washington road, 1990s

Longtime residents of these cities were not always welcoming. As outsiders swelled their city's population, local citizens feared they too would soon have to cope with smog and traffic jams. Taking a lesson from Los Angeles, Portland, Oregon, and other western cities began trying to keep from growing too fast.

In the late twentieth century westerners on the farms in the Great Plains were also on the move. By the 1980s few small farms could survive on the Plains because the cost of equipment and supplies was too high, and the selling price of their crops was too low. Looking for new opportunities, many young men and women left the region, often for western cities.

On the other hand, another western industry—tourism—has continued to flourish. Some 600 million visitors from all over the world come to the national parks and forests of the West annually. Each year more tourists flock to see the beautiful scenery for which the region has always been famous.

Enjoying the unspoiled wilderness of Yellowstone or the Grand Canyon, visitors can almost pretend that the West has been untouched by time. The real West, though, has always been a place of change. Throughout recorded history, it has been a land of many peoples, each with different ideas on how to make the region its home. Navajo farmers, Lakota hunters, conquistadors, mountain men, gold miners, homesteaders, cowboys, factory workers, suburbanites—all came with dreams for themselves and for the land. For many, the region's promise remains as strong as ever. To this day, when thinking of the future, Americans find themselves turning to the West.

Iranians, and Cambodians. The children in the city's public schools speak more than 80 different languages.

While Los Angeles was attracting new Americans, many older city residents left. Tired of freeways and suburban sprawl, some Californians moved to other western cities such as Denver and Salt Lake City, which had not experienced such rapid growth.

INDEX

RECOMMENDED RESOURCES

GENERAL SOURCES

Books

Duncan, Dayton. *People of the West.* Boston: Little Brown, 1996.

————. *The West: An Illustrated History for Children.* Boston: Little Brown, 1996.

Freedman, Russell. *Children of the Wild West.* New York: Clarion Books, 1983.

Katz, William Loren. *Black Pioneers: An Untold Story.* New York: Atheneum, 1999.

Ketchum, Liza. *Into a New Country: Eight Remarkable Women of the West.* Boston: Little Brown, 2000.

Sakurai, Gail. *Asian-Americans in the Old West.* New York: Children's Press, 2000.

Web sites

The West, www.pbs.org/weta/thewest

Women of the West Museum, www.wowmuseum.org

Photographs of the American West (section of the National Archives site), www.nara.gov/nara/nn/ nns/amwest. html

Videotapes

Burns, Ken, prod. "The West." Alexandria, VA: PBS Home Video. 9 videotapes, 707 min., 1996.

FIRST PERSON ACCOUNTS

Books

Colbert, David. *Eyewitness to the American West.* New York: Viking, 1998.

Miller, Lee, ed. *From the Heart: Voices of the American Indian.* New York: Knopf, 1995.

Schlissel, Lillian. *Women's Diaries of the Westward Journey.* New York: Schocken Books, 1982.

Wexler, Sanford. *Westward Expansion.* New York: Facts on File, 1991.

CHAPTER 1

Books

Arnold, Caroline. *The Ancient Cliff Dwellers of Mesa Verde.* New York: Clarion Books, 1992.

Liptak, Karen. *Indians of the Pacific Northwest.* New York: Facts on File, 1991.

Powell, Suzanne. *The Pueblos.* New York: Franklin Watts, 1993.

Snow, Dean. *The Archaeology of North America.* New York: Chelsea House Publishers, 1989.

CHAPTER 2

Books

Baldwin, Louis. *Intruders Within: Pueblo Resistance to Spanish Rule and the Revolt of 1680.* New York: Franklin Watts, 1995.

Freedman, Russell. *Buffalo Hunt.* New York: Holiday House, 1988.

Morriss, Roger. *Captain Cook and His Exploration of the Pacific.* Hauppauge, NY: Barron's Educational Series, 1998.

Van Steenwyk, Elizabeth. *The California Missions.* New York: Franklin Watts, 1995.

CHAPTER 3

Books

Allen, John Logan. *Jedediah Smith and the Mountain Men of the American West.* New York: Chelsea House, 1991.

Hoig, Stan. *Night of the Cruel Moon: Cherokee Removal and the Trail of Tears.* New York: Facts on File, 1996.

Stefoff, Rebecca. *Children of the Westward Trail.* Brookfield, CT: Millbrook Press, 1996.

Sullivan, George. *Alamo!* New York: Scholastic, 1997.

Web sites

Lewis and Clark, www.pbs.org/lewisandclark

The Oregon Trail, www.isu. edu/~trinmich/Oregontrail.html

CHAPTER 4

Books

Anderson, Peter. *The Pony Express.* New York: Children's Press, 1996.

Ketchum, Liza. *The Gold Rush.* Boston: Little Brown, 1996.

Rudolf, Claire, and Jane G. Haigh. *Children of the Gold Rush.* Boulder, CO: Roberts Rinehart, 1999.

Zeinert, Karen. *Tragic Prelude: Bleeding Kansas.* North Haven, CT: Shoe String Press, 2000.

Web sites

The Gold Rush, www.pbs.org/goldrush

"California as I Saw It": First Person Narratives of California's Early Years, 1849–1900 (section of the Library of Congress site), memory.loc.gov/ ammem/cbhtml/cbhome.html

CHAPTER 5

Books

Cox, Clinton. *The Forgotten Heroes: The Story of the Buffalo Soldiers.* New York: Scholastic, 1993.

Terry, Michael Bad Hand. *Daily Life in a Plains Indian Village, 1868.* New York: Clarion Books, 1999.

Viola, Herman J., ed. *It Is a Good Day to Die: Indian Eyewitnesses Tell the Story of the Battle of Little Big Horn.* New York: Crown Publishing, 1998.

Wormser, Richard. *The Iron Horse: How Railroads Changed America.* New York: Walker, 1993.

Videotapes

Ades, Lisa, and Ric Burns, prods. "The Way West." Alexandria, VA: PBS Home Video. 4 videotapes, 360 min., 1995.

CHAPTER 6

Books

Freedman, Russell. *Cowboys of the Wild West.* New York: Clarion Books, 1990.

Herda, D. J. *Outlaws of the American West.* Brookfield, CT: Millbrook Press, 1995.

O'Neill, Laurie A. *Wounded Knee: The Death of a Dream.* Brookfield, CT: Millbrook Press, 1993.

Smith, Carter, ed. *The Legendary Wild West.* Brookfield, CT: Millbrook Press, 1992.

Web sites

Buffalo Bill Historical Center, www. bbhc.org

National Cowboy Hall of Fame and Western Heritage Center, www.cowboyhalloffame.org

CHAPTER 7

Books

De Ruiz, Dana Catherine, and Richard Larios. *La Causa: The Migrant Farmworkers' Story.* Austin, TX: Raintree Steck-Vaughn, 1993.

Stanley, Jerry. *Children of the Dust Bowl: The True Story of the School at Weedpatch Camp.* New York: Crown Publishing, 1992.

Tunnell, Michael O., and George W. Chilcoat. *The Children of Topaz: The Story of a Japanese-American Internment Camp Based on a Classroom Diary.* New York: Holiday House, 1996.

Web sites

Voices from the Dust Bowl (section of the Library of Congress site), memory. loc.gov/ammem/afctshtml/tshome.html

PHOTO CREDITS

KEY: T (top); B (bottom); L (left); R (right).

Page 4: Yosemite National Park Collections; **6:** # 326529. American Museum of Natural History Library; **8:** Jack Parsons; **9L:** Brooklyn Museum of Art, Museum Expedition 1906, Museum Collection Fund 06.331.8197; **9TR:** # 278574. American Museum of Natural History Library; **9TL:** # 286822. American Museum of Natural History Library; **10:** Richard A. Cooke/CORBIS; **11T:** David Muench; **11B:** Jerry Jacka, Courtesy National Park Service; **12:** Field Museum of Natural History; **13:** School of American Research, IAF.C253; **15T:** Phoebe Hearst Museum of Anthropology and the Regents of the University of California; **15B:** Brooklyn Museum of Art, Museum Expedition 1906, Museum Collection Fund 06.331.8198; **16:** Burke Museum of Natural History and Culture, Catalog #955, Chief Shakes' rattle, Nanya.aayi Tlingit Clan, Wrangell, Alaska; **17T:** *Grand Potlatch at Fort Hope, Fraser River, 1859* by Frederick Whymper; **17B:** Burke Museum of Natural History and Culture, Catalog #1989–11/1. "En-tee-teeq'w," Salmon Sculpture by Stephen T. Noyes, Colville Confederated Tribes/Puyallup Tribe; **18:** Chilkat Coat by Mrs. Benson, Tlingit, Yakutat. ©2001 Portland Art Museum, Portland, OR. Axel Ramussen Collection, purchased with the Indian Collection Subscription Fund; **19T:** Library of Congress; **19B:** San Diego Museum of Man. Photo, John Oldenkamp; **20:** Arizona State Museum, University of Arizona. Photo, Helgo Teiwes; **22:** Lee Boltin Picture Library; **23T:** Remington Art Memorial; **24:** Detail, Ben Wittick, Museum of New Mexico, # 16039; **25:** # 286821. American Museum of Natural History Library; **26:** Manuscripts and Archives Division, The New York Public Library; **27:** Smithsonian American Art Museum, Washington, DC/Art Resource, NY; **28T:** Bancroft Library. University of California, Berkeley. SF309 G7 M25 1769 pl.22; **28B:** Museum of the South Dakota State Historical Society, Pierre, SD; **29:** Rare Books Division, New York Public Library, Astor, Lenox and Tilden Foundations; **30:** National Anthropological Archives, National Museum of Natural History Smithsonian Institution. # 3700; **31:** Detail, George Catlin, *Chief of the Taensa Indians Receiving La Salle. March 20, 1682,* Paul Mellon Collection, Photograph © 2001 Board of Trustees, National Gallery of Art, Washington, DC; **32T:** Ferdinand Deppe oil painting of Mission San Gabriel, 1832. Santa Barbara Mission Archive-Library; **32B:** Mosqueda's portrait of Fr. Junipero Serra. Santa Barbara Mission Archive-Library; **34:** Burke Museum of Natural History and Culture, # 4652, "Wooden Bowl, Makah."; **35T:** John Webber, *The Inside of a House in Nootka Sound,* n.d., engraving on paper, 22.2 x 36.8 cm. Collection of Glenbow Museum. CN: 57.51.3 PHN: 4606; **35B:** Lee Boltin Picture Library; **36:** Denver Public Library, Western History Department. Detail, W.H. Jackson; **38L:** Independence National Historical Park Collection; **38R:** Collection of The New-York Historical Society. # 51322; **39:** Missouri Historical Society, St. Louis. Clark Family Papers; **40:** Charles M. Russell, *Lewis and Clark on the Lower Columbia,* 1905, watercolor on paper. Amon Carter Museum, Fort Worth, TX, 1961.195; **41L:** Missouri Historical Society, St. Louis. Clark Family Collection; **41R:** # 299396 Photo: R. E. Logan. American Museum of Natural History Library; **42T:** Missouri Historical Society, St. Louis; **42B:** Culver Pictures; **43T:** Missouri Historical Society, St. Louis; **43B:** Bancroft Library. University of California, Berkeley. 1963.002.1529-FR; **44:** Rare Books Division, New York Public Library, Astor, Lenox and Tilden Foundations; **45:** Smithsonian American Art Museum, Washington, DC/Art Resource, NY; **46T:** Woolaroc Museum, Bartlesville, OK; **46B:** National Museum of the American Indian/Smithsonian Institution. (# 30929); **47:** California History Room, California State Library, Sacramento, CA; **48:** State Historical Society of Wisconsin. # WHi X32 20425; **49:** Oregon Historical Society, # OrHi 87748; **50:** Fair Street Pictures; **51T:** Kansas State Historical Society; **51B:** Oregon Historical Society, # OrHi 96320; **52:** Lane County Historical Museum; **53:** *Handcart Pioneers* by CCA Christensen © Intellectual Reserve, Inc. Museum of Church History and Art. Used by Permission; **54T:** Texas Memorial Museum, # 1776–1; **55:** San Jacinto Museum of History, Houston; **56–57:** Library of Congress; **58:** Collection of W. Bruce Lundberg; **60:** "A Gold Hunter on his Way to California, via St. Louis,"ca. 1849. Henry R. Robinson. California Historical Society, FN-16057; **61:** Chicago Historical Society, ICHi-31048; **62:** Bancroft Library. University of California, Berkeley. 1963.002.0266-B; **63:** California History Room, California State Library, Sacramento, CA; **64:** Collection of The New-York Historical Society. # 48381; **65T:** Isaac W. Baker/Oakland Museum of California, gift of anonymous owner; **65BL:** Cover of *Life and Adventures of Joaquin Murieta,* by Yellow Bird (John Rollin Ridge), published by the University of Oklahoma Press. © 1955; **66:** Denver Public Library, Western History Collection. Photo: Thomas M. McKee; **67T:** National Archives; **67B:** Wyoming State Archives, Department of State Parks and Cultural Resources; **68:** Henry Ford Museum & Greenfield Village. P.DPC.030655; **69:** Bancroft Library. University of California, Berkeley. 1963.002.0311 -D; **71:** The Walters Art Museum, Baltimore; **72:** Library of Congress; **74:** Boston Athenaeum; **75:** Kansas State Historical Society; **76:** Detail, Oakland Museum of California; **78T:** Library of Congress; **78B:** Kansas State Historical Society; **79:** Archives and Manuscript Division of the Oklahoma Historical Society; **80:** National Anthropological Archives, National Museum of Natural History Smithsonian Institution. # 3238 E; **81:** National Anthropological Archives, National Museum of Natural History Smithsonian Institution. # 1746 A-2; **82:** National Archives; **83T:** Panhandle-Plains Historical Museum; **83B:** Colorado Historical Society; F40341; **84:** Collection of The New-York Historical Society. # 67962; **85T:** Nebraska State Historical Society; **85B:** Kansas State Historical Society; **86:** University of Southern California, Regional History Collection; **87:** Nebraska State Historical Society; **88:** Library of Congress; **89:** Nebraska State Historical Society; **90:** Detail, Bancroft Library, University of California; **91:** Detail, The Andrew J. Russell Collection, Oakland Museum of California; **92:** Wadsworth Atheneum. Bequest of Elizabeth Hart Jarvis Colt; **93:** Union Pacific Historical Collection; **94:** Library of Congress; **95:** Yellowstone National Park; **96:** Union Pacific Historical Collection; **97B:** DeGolyer Library, Southern Methodist University, Dallas, TX, Robert Benecke [Ag1982:0086:060]; **98T:** The Southwest Museum, Los Angeles; **98B:** Monroe County Historical Commission; **99:** Library of Congress; **100:** Archives and Manuscript Division of the Oklahoma Historical Society; **103:** Detail, The Anschutz Collection. Photo: William J. O'Connor; **104T:** Denver Public Library, Western History Department; **104B:** Colorado Historical Society. Photo, O. T. Davis; **105:** Nebraska State Historical Society; **107T:** Buffalo Bill Historical Center, Cody, WY, Vincent Mercaldo Collection, P.71.659.2; **107B:** Western History Collections, University of Oklahoma Library; **108:** Denver Public Library, Western History Department; **110:** Western History Collections, University of Oklahoma Library; **111:** Kansas State Historical Society; **113:** Cumberland County Historical Society, Carlisle, PA; **114:** Nebraska State Historical Society; **115:** Library of Congress; **116:** Wyoming State Archives, Department of State Parks and Cultural Resources; **117:** Bettmann/CORBIS; **118:** Washington Tourism Division; **120–121T:** Library of Congress; **121B:** U. S. Geological Survey; **122:** Library of Congress; **123:** Casa Del Desierto, Fred Harvey Collection. Special Collections, University of Arizona Library; **124–126:** Library of Congress; **127:** Copyright the Dorothea Lange Collection, Oakland Museum of California, City of Oakland. Gift of Paul S. Taylor; **128:** Bettmann/CORBIS; **129–131:** National Archives; **132T:** Hulton-Deutsch Collection/CORBIS; **132B:** Herald Examiner Collection/Los Angeles Public Library; **133:** Bettmann/CORBIS; **134:** Photofest; **135:** Bettmann/CORBIS; **136:** Sally Anderson-Bruce; **137:** Joseph Sohm, ChromoSohm Inc./CORBIS; **138:** Joe Viesti/ The Viesti Collection